The Layman's G

GDPR

for

Small Medium Business

European Union

(General Data Protection Regulation)

Copyright © Alasdair Gilchrist 2017

Part I – layman's concise guide to GDPR Compliance 9

Chapter I - Introduction to GDPR 9

   Data Protective Directive (DPD) 10

   Introduction to GDPR Definitions 12

   Controllers vs. Processors 12

      Data Subjects 15

      Personal Data 15

      DPA/Supervisory Body 16

      Quick Overview to GDPR Compliance 17

      Territorial application 19

      Consent 19

      Rights of data subjects 19

      72 hour data breach notification 19

      Increased compliance obligations for controllers 19

      Direct compliance obligations for processors 19

      Appointing a DPO 20

      Cross-Border Data Transfers 20

      Remedies and sanctions 20

      Transitional provisions 20

Chapter II – GDPR Principles and New Articles 22

      Increased Territorial Scope 23

      GDPR's expansion of Processor responsibility 25

      GDPR's expanded concept of consent 27

      Data Subject Rights 30

      Breach Notification 30

      Right to Access 31

      Right to be Forgotten 36

      Right to Object 39

Data Portability 40

Privacy by Design 44

Transparency 46

Data Protection Officers 49

Restrictions 54

Penalties 55

Part II - Assessing GDPR Readiness & Compliance 56

  Chapter III – GDPR Threats & Opportunities 57

    Threats 57

    Opportunities 58

  Accountability 64

    What are the accountability principles? 64

    What do I need to record? 66

  Awareness 67

    The twelve principles of the GDPR 67

Chapter V – Data Governance & Privacy Management 74

  The requirement for Consent 74

    GDPR requires parental consent for processing children's personal data 82

    Other Provisions where explicit consent is required 83

    Information Provided at Data Collection 83

    Breach & Notification 84

    Data Subject Profiling 86

  Defining profiling 87

    Notice and access 91

    Data impact assessments for controllers engaged in profiling 91

    Legitimate Interests & Direct Marketing 92

Chapter VI – Performing a Privacy Impact Assessment 93

Assessing GDPR Readiness 94

Privacy Impact Assessment 97

PIA vs. DIPA 97

Chapter VII – Deriving Business Opportunities via Compliance 109

So where can these advantages come from? 109

GDPR Enforcement 112

The GDPR's emphasis on data security 113

Harmonizing of Organizational Processes and Procedures 115

Harmonization of EU privacy laws 115

Lead authority one-stop shop 116

Data breach reporting 117

Chapter VIII - Brexit and the GDPR 119

Part III – A Review of the GDPR Articles 123

Study of the GDPR Articles 123

Article 1 - Aims and objectives of the law 125

Article 2 – Material Scope 127

Article – 3 Territorial Scope 130

Article 4 – Definitions 133

Article – 5 Fair, lawful and transparent processing 140

Article – 6 Lawfulness 143

Article 7: Conditions for consent 150

Article 8: Conditions applicable to child's consent in relation to information society services 157

Article 9: Processing of special categories of personal data 158

Article 10: Processing of data relating to criminal convictions and offences 160

Article 11: Processing which does not require identification 160

Section 1: Transparency and Modalities 161

Section 2: Information and Access to Data 161

Section 5: Restrictions 161

    Article 12: Transparent information, communication and modalities for the exercise of the rights of the data subject 161

    Article 13: Information to be provided where personal data are collected from the data subject 164

    Article 15: Right of access by the data subject 166

    Article 16: Right to rectification 167

    Article 17: Right to erasure ('right to be forgotten') 168

    Article 18: Right to restriction of processing 169

    Article 19: Notification obligation 169

    Article 20: Right to data portability 170

Section 4: Right to object and automated individual decision making 171

    Article 21: Right to object 171

    Article 22: Automated individual decision-making, including profiling 174

Section 5: Restrictions 175

    Article 23: Restrictions 175

Section 1: General Obligations 175

    Article 24: Responsibility of the controller 176

    Article 25: Data protection by design and by default 177

    Article 26: Joint controllers 178

    Article 27: Representatives of controllers not established in the Union 180

    Article 28 - Appointment of processors 180

    Article 29: Processing under the authority of the controller or processor 181

    Article 30: Records of processing activities 182

Article 31: Cooperation with the supervisory authority 183

Article 32: Security of processing 183

Article 33: Notification of a personal data breach to the supervisory authority 184

Article 34: Communication of a personal data breach to the data subject 185

Article 35: Data protection impact assessment 187

Article 36: Prior Consultation 188

Article 37: Designation of the data protection officer 189

Article 38: Position of the data protection officer 190

Article 39: Tasks of the data protection officer 191

Article 40: Codes of Conduct 193

Article 41: Monitoring of approved codes of conduct 194

Article 42: Certification 196

Article 43: Certification Bodies 196

Article 44: General Principle for transfer 198

Article 45: Transfers of the basis of an adequacy decision 200

Article 46: Transfers subject to appropriate safeguards 201

Article 47: Binding corporate rules 204

Article 48: Transfers or disclosures not authorised by union law 206

Article 49: Derogations for specific situations 207

Article 50: International cooperation for the protection of personal data 211

International and Third Party Cooperation 211

Article 51: Supervisory Authority 213

Article 52: Independence 214

Article 53: General conditions for the members of the supervisory authority 215

Article 54: Rules on the establishment of the supervisory Authority 215

Section 2: Competence, Tasks, and Powers 216

Article 55: Competence 216

Article 56: Competence of the lead supervisory authority 216

Article 57: Tasks 217

Article 58: Powers 217

Article 59: Activity Reports 218

Article 60: Cooperation between the lead supervisory authority and the other supervisory authorities concerned 219

Article 61: Mutual Assistance 219

Article 62: Joint operations of supervisory authorities 220

Article 63: Consistency mechanism 220

Article 64: Opinion of the Board 221

Article 65: Dispute resolution by the Board 222

Article 66: Urgency Procedure 223

Article 67: Exchange of information 223

Article 68 – European Data Protection Board 224

Article 69 – Independence 225

Article 70 –Tasks of the Board 225

Article 71- Reports 225

Article 72- Procedure 226

Article 73- Chair 226

Activity 74 – Tasks of the Chair 226

Article 75 – Secretariat 227

Activity 76 – Confidentiality 227

Article 77: Right to lodge a complaint with a supervisory authority 228

Article 78: Right to an effective judicial remedy against a supervisory authority 229

Article 79: Right to an effective judicial remedy against a controller or processor 230

Article 80: Representation of data subjects 230

Article 81: Suspension of proceedings 231

Article 82: Right to compensation and liability 232

Article 83: General conditions for imposing administrative fines 234

Article 84: Penalties 236

Article 85: Processing and freedom of expression and information 237

Article 86: Processing and public access to official documents 238

Article 87: Processing of the national identification number 239

Article 88: Processing in the context of employment 239

Article 89: Safeguards and derogations relating to processing for archiving purposes in the public interest, scientific or historical research purposes or statistical purposes 240

Article 90: Obligations of secrecy 240

Article 91: Existing data protection rules of churches and religious associations 241

Article 94: Repeal of Directive 95/46/EC 243

Article 95: Relationship with Directive 2002/58/EC 244

Article 96: Relationship with previously concluded Agreements 244

Article 97: Commission Reports 245

Article 98: Review of other union legal acts on data protection 245

Article 99: Entry intro force and application 246

Part I – layman's concise guide to GDPR Compliance

Chapter I - Introduction to GDPR

To set the scene for the introduction of the General Data Protection Regulations (GDPR) we will first spend this chapter considering the present legislation and how it affects business today. The current data privacy laws in the EU member states vary quite considerably as each member state has applied the EU Data Protection Directive 96/46/EC as the basis for their own data privacy laws. This is because the Data Protection Directive 95/46/EC was only a Directive and as such is only recommended guidelines rather than a regulation or mandatory articles of law. The EU GDPR on the other hand is a regulation so will be brought into law in its entirety in each member state. Hence for the first time there will be a common data privacy law across all member states of the EU Community.

The fundamental importance of the current EU Data Protection Directive 96/46/EU is that it addresses an important EU principle that of the right to privacy for all EU residents. This principle is extremely important as it is considered in the EU to be a fundamental human right. Indeed the right to privacy, was adopted back in 1950 and subsequently introduced to the EU Human Rights Conference in 1998 introduced under Article 8 (Right to Privacy) in the Human Rights Act (HRA 1998) in European law.

In the UK for example it is important to consider that the present law under the EU-Harmonized Data Protection Act of 1998 is based upon the EU Data Protection Directive of 1995 and that all member states of the EU have similar laws based upon the Data Protection Directive which are applied within their own legal structure. The flexibility allowed when implementing the Directive however has resulted in a disparate set of privacy laws throughout the European Community, which has been far from ideal.

Ironically, the Data Protection Directive 95/46/EC of 24 October 1995 were the European Union's answer to the existing division of privacy regulations across the EU. Hence, its major goals included the harmonization of data protection laws and the transfer of personal data to "third countries" outside of the Union. It established independent public authorities called Data Protection Authorities (DPAs) in each member state in order to supervise the application of this directive and serve as the regulatory body for interactions with businesses and citizens. The DPD also provided for the allowance of transfers of personal data to third countries, on the condition that said countries were authorized as having adequate levels of protection for the data. This was an important point as third party countries would be required being guaranteed to be comparable to those protections within the EU – for example share a comparable ethos regards data privacy. Overall, the directive has worked well despite creaking with age and stays true to the original recommendations and the core concepts of privacy as a fundamental human right.

Data Protective Directive (DPD)

The DPD is what exists today - variants of the Data Protective Directive (DPD) implemented in each member state in the UK for example it is called the Data Protection Act.

However as the DPD is now over twenty years old and was drafted long before the prevalence of the web, mobile data and social media it was struggling to find relevance in the modern world. Consequently, a new revision was proposed and the UK amongst others was a major driver behind the drafting of a new General Data Protection Regulation back in 2013, which would have relevance in the modern internet era. Therefore even though the UK may leave the EU soon after GDPR becomes statutory across all the EU member states in 2018 it will still be law in the UK and UK based businesses will need to be compliant. Furthermore, even if the UK Government was to remove the regulations from the statute books - which is highly unlikely as they contributed so much to the draft - any business wishing to conduct business within the EU single market that necessitates the collection and processing of EU citizens personal data would still require to be GDPR compliant. This is an important point as it is necessary to understand that the territorial scope of the GDPR has changed and any organization even those with no EU establishment will be required to be GDPR compliant if they supply products or services which collect the private data or monitor the behaviour of EU residents.

The importance of data privacy as a fundamental right within the EU for all citizens is a principle which the EU holds dearly and as such plays a large part in the revised GDPR. The previous Data Protection Directive was drafted way back in 1995 and came into law in most EU states in 1998 but that was only at the dawn of the internet and long before ecommerce and the web had become ubiquitous. Therefore the adapted EU laws in many countries was not sufficient to face the privacy challenges which came about through the proliferation of web browsing, social media, cloud computing services, ecommerce and importantly the invasive nature of direct advertising to the user. Similarly many felt that the current regulations did not address the business models and practices of the vast internet sized companies that harvested EU citizens' personal data and transferred it to offshore locations out with the EU.

The Safe Harbour, was one such transatlantic agreement drawn up to allow US based internet companies to transfer EU citizens data out with the community borders despite there being little guarantee of its privacy. Indeed when challenged in court the Safe Harbour was found to be unsafe and struck down. The Court of Justice EU declared the Safe Harbour scheme for EU-US data transfers to be invalid. While Safe Harbour was not the only way to transfer data to the US from the EU, around 4,500 companies relied on this framework as their main legal basis for transfers.

The case against the Safe Harbour was originally brought about by Austrian student Max Schrems, following the NSA revelations by Edward Snowden. The CJEU ruled that the US public authorities were not only outside of the scope of Safe Harbour, but also support conflicting laws that prevail over the scheme in certain circumstances.

The Safe Harbour decisions in 2015 came after work started on the revision of privacy regulations which began in 2013 so did not bring about GDPR but the decision does go to demonstrate why a revision and update of EU data privacy laws were required to meet the changing demands of the internet era.

In order to understand the changes that the GDPR will bring for businesses operating within the EU market upon its implementation into law in May 2018 we need to consider what the UK and the other EU member states already use as their directive for data privacy protection.

Introduction to GDPR Definitions

In order to understand many of the concepts and articles within the GDPR we need to first understand some of the roles to which the law applies. The main roles referred to in the existing Data Protection Directive and the GDPR are Data Controllers, Data Processors and Data Subjects and of importance is the data referenced refers only to a subject's Personal Data. Therefore to understand the articles within the context of the regulations we need to have as a starting point a clear definition and hence an understanding of what constitutes a Controller, Processor and Subject with regards handling the subject's Personal Data.

Controllers vs. Processors

The major differentiator between a Data Controller and a Data Processor is that the Controller stipulates what data is to be collected for what purpose and how it will be processed. The Processor on the other hand is the entity charged with collecting, storing and processing the data on behalf of a Controller. An example of this in these days of cloud storage and computing would be for instance in the case of an Insurance Company or a Bank that stipulates what personal data should be collected for a policy quotation or for a loan application. They will determine the criteria for collecting the personal data and stipulate the conditions for managing the data such as the period it is to be stored for and the conditions for its disposal. The processor, the cloud service provider, will then be responsible for undertaking the collection, physical storage and data management for the duration of the data lifecycle.

In the DPD and GDPR, the roles of the Controllers and Processors are very distinctly separated however in practice many large companies and enterprises may be both Controllers and Processors as they serve both functions in-house. This is of course true of SMBs, (Small Medium Business), as they are often dealing with only small manageable amounts of customers' personal data in Financial systems or in a CRM (Customer Relationship Management) database. Therefore it is important to clearly define your role within the GDPR, for example are you the controller, a processor or both. The key component when determining the role of an organization is the Subject Data, which is defined as being personal identifiable information (PII) and those responsible for the governance of the data are Controllers and those tasked with managing and handling the data are Processors regardless of whether they are a single or independent corporate/business entities.

A key distinguishing measure for determining whether an organization is acting as a controller or as a processor or both is that under the current directive a processor must only process the data at the explicit request of and for the explicit purpose stated by the controller and generally this takes the form of a contract. Before we proceed it is important to define what is meant by processing, as under the Directive and the GDPR it is loosely defined to cover just about anything such as collecting, handling, cataloguing, storing, securing, transferring, analysing, it can cover just about any operation on the personal data in your possession. Hence, should the organisation acting as the data processor expand their role to processing the data for a purpose outside of the contractual agreement with their customer (the controller) say for their own analytics or other purpose then they have crossed the fine line and would then be considered to be acting as a controller.

An important practical distinction between being recognized as the Data Controller or the Processor is how the roles are viewed under current legislation. Data Controllers do have statutory obligations under the current Data Protection Directives such as they must have a written legal contract with a Data Processor. Furthermore there is an onus on the Data Controller to take reasonable steps to ensure that the Data Processor is acting in accordance with the security conditions laid out in the contract such as through performing regular audits. Therefore presently the regulatory and statutory obligations fall upon the Data Controller.

Importantly under the current Data Protection Directive, it is very advantageous to be a Data Processor as there are no statutory or regulatory obligations on Data Processors under the current directive. This means that in practice the only control on Data Processors is under any contractual agreement stipulated with the Data Controller, so control is contractual rather than statutory leaving Data Processors free from any threat of fines from a regulatory body. Hence so long as a Data Processor keeps a clear distinction between their activities and those of a Data Controller they have a free reign to operate as they please.

Consequently, one of the purposes of the GDPR is to rectify this anomaly and bring Data Processors under direct regulatory control with direct statutory obligations albeit not as stringent as those for a Data Controller. Therefore under GDPR we will find that Data Processors will have to show clear capability dealing with handling data security, managing sub-processors, diligent record keeping and timely breach reporting. There are other obligations under GDPR, which we will discuss later. For now it will suffice to understand that the Data Processor will be going from basically zero liability under current directives to some hefty liabilities to regulators, data subjects and even to their Data Controllers if they are found to have breached regulations. Indeed the Data Processors could find themselves liable for failure to comply with statutory obligations as well as contractual obligations, a double liability. Furthermore they could be liable for unlimited compensation to Data Subjects which is high risk as they have no means to contractually limit the exposure through a contract.

Data Subjects

A Data Subject is defined as the subject of the personal data being collected and stored by the Controller and Processor. The Data Subject provides the personal data requested by a Data Controller hence the direct relationship is between the Data Controller and the Data Subject as it is the responsibility of the Data Controller to stipulate what personal data should be collected and for what specific purpose. For example a data subject is an EU resident who is supplying personal data to or being monitored by an organization.

Personal Data

The definition of Personal Data or PII (Personal Identifiable Information) is very important as it is the protection of this specific type of data that is the purpose of the regulations. Personal data is determined to be data or information that can be used on its own or in conjunction with other data that the controller may or may not currently possess but could well do in the future, which could be used to identify a living person. However, there is another tier of personal data under the DPD, which is also present and expanded upon under GDPR which is called Sensitive Personal Data. This category of sensitive data relates to information which could be used to determine an individual's racial or ethnic origin, their sexual orientation, their physical or mental health, criminal convictions, trade union membership and even their political or religious persuasions. The GDPR supports all the categories of Sensitive Personal Data listed under the DPD and adds some other sensitive data categories pertaining to children, as well as genetic and biometric data which we will see later.

Currently the Data Protection Directives state 8 key principles of data privacy, hence personal data (PII) must:

1. be processed fairly and lawfully
2. only be processed for one or more specified and lawful purposes and not further processed in a manner incompatible with those purposes

3. be relevant, adequate but not excessive for the purpose
4. be accurate and where necessary kept up to date
5. not be processed for longer than is necessary
6. be in accordance with data subjects rights
7. Be protected by appropriate technical and organizational security measures
8. not be transferred outside of the EEA unless that country ensures an adequate level of protection for personal data

These are the main principles behind current EU data protection and privacy directives to EU Member States and forms the basis for the pivacy laws. Some of these principles have received a lot of press lately for example item No 8 which was the restricted transfer of EU subjects personal data outwith the EEA created a conflict with some of the internet giant tech companies who do not share the EU's belief that privacy is a basic human right and not a commodity to be harvested and traded on the open market.

DPA/Supervisory Body

The DPA is the authority tasked with enforcing the law in order to protect the privacy of personal data and ensuring action is taken against those that fail to comply with the Data Protection Laws. Unfortunately because the DPD was implemented in a variety of flavours across the EU Member States this disparity in the law causes some conflict between Member State DPAs who were working to different regulations. Consequently the GDPR strives to mitigate much of this conflict by setting a community wide regulation that will be implemented in its entirety across all Member States.

Now that we have a basic high level understanding of the reasons why the GDPR has been introduced, what it is, and learned some of the key roles within the GDPR articles we can move on to consider what is new within the articles and how they differ from the current Data Protection Directive and how we can prepare for the application of the GDPR in May 2018.

Quick Overview to GDPR Compliance

These 10 steps will ease the pain of compliance with the General Data Protection Regulation, the EU's new privacy law that goes into effect in a little over a year.

If your organization does business with Europe, or more specifically does anything with the personal data of EU citizens, you're going to fall under the auspice of the new regulation so that will mean preparing for the General Data Protection Regulation (GDPR).

For many organizations, that already comply with the EU directives and have competent data governance procedures in place this will be relatively straightforward. On the other hand for organizations that currently do not fall under the current scope of the EU directives and for those with poor data governance this is going to be a tedious exercise. However, even if you have implemented processes and technologies to meet current regulations, there is still work to be done to steer clear of penalties. And, as you might expect, infringement carries heavy fines: maximum of €20 million or 4 percent of your worldwide annual gross revenue, depending on the category of the violation.

The regulation comes into effect on May 25, 2018, at which point organizations will be held accountable – there will be no further transitional period as organisations have already had two years it will become effective immediately on that date in May 2018. Surprisingly, although there has been much activity and interest from Law Firms and large enterprises along with the obvious candidates the tech giants, small medium businesses seem to be less enthused by the potential threat of the GDPR. Therefore it's hard to say exactly how these smaller organizations are doing, perhaps many simply do not realise that by collecting and storing EU residents personal data – even on that legacy CRM system in the corner – they will be classified as a controller. This lack of awareness may be the biggest threat of all to SME (small medium enterprises), as they may not even know that they are covered by the new GDPR and currently in May 2017 with exactly a year to go it doesn't appear that too many are ready.

For one thing, preparing for GDPR is likely to be a cross-functional exercise, as the Board, senior executives, legal, Security, Risk and Compliance, IT, DevOps, Sales &Marketing all have a part to play. Some organizations will need to adopt new roles and responsibilities, such as appointing a data protection officer and nominating representatives within the EU to be the required points of contact.

For SME organizations that are just beginning the journey towards GDPR compliance their quest starts by having employees attend awareness training to learn about the best practices for implementing GDPR. Awareness training for all relevant staff can help create a culture of data privacy and diligent data governance throughout the organization and that alone can go a long way in mitigating the threat of costly fines, which, depending on the level of GDPR infringement, can amount to 4% of your organization's worldwide annual gross revenue for the previous year.

Interestingly SMEs most common complaint is directly related to poor data governance as they often are simple unable to determine where the personal data of EU citizens physically resides, the categories of personal data they control or process, and therefore they cannot know reliably how and by whom it is accessed, and how it is secured. Retrospectively introducing diligent data governance will be a challenge for many and it does need to be addressed retrospectively as GDPR applies to legacy as well as new products and services so organizations will have to review all their data assets and systems for compliance. In addition, processes for consent, sharing, access control, incident detection and response, and breach notification will also need review or implementation.

In order to appreciate the scale of the challenge – for some this will be trivial for other monumental – we need to consider the main GDPR changes to the current Directive that may be considered to have a negative impact on current operational practices.

Territorial application

First and most importantly is that the GDPR territorial scope has expanded to meet the challenges of the internet era. Hence the GDPR now applies to non-EU organisations if they: (i) offer goods or services to EU residents; or (ii) monitor the behaviour of EU residents. Many organisations that are not subject to existing EU data protection law will be subject to the GDPR, especially online businesses

Consent

Data processing of EU residents' personal data requires being lawful the individual's Consent and that becomes harder for organisations to obtain and rely on. Notably, the GDPR states that consent is not valid where there is a "clear imbalance" between the controller and the data subject i.e. between Employer and Employee.

Rights of data subjects

The EU regulation has expanded and strengthened the rights of data subjects (e.g., the right to object) and some new rights are created (e.g., the right to data portability) others are formalized and codified (e.g., the right to be forgotten)

72 hour data breach notification

A significant challenge to organizations will be that the GDPR requires businesses to report data breaches to the relevant DPA within 72 hours of detection. For many organisations, radical changes to internal reporting structures will be needed

Increased compliance obligations for controllers

The GDPR imposes new and increased compliance obligations on controllers (e.g., implementing appropriate policies, keeping records of processing activities, privacy by design and by default, etc)

Direct compliance obligations for processors

Under the GDPR, processors will now have direct legal compliance obligations, and DPAs can take enforcement action against processors

Appointing a DPO

Organisations that regularly and systematically monitor data subjects, or process Sensitive Personal Data on a large scale, must appoint a Data Protection Officer

Cross-Border Data Transfers

This may me a burden or a boon as the GDPR provides for greater consistency in the application of BCRs in all Member States but it does enforce stricter compliance rules. The GDPR does though suggest a number of alternate data transfer mechanisms (e.g., adherence to an approved Code of Conduct, Certification, Model Contracts, Ad Hoc arrangements, amongst others)

Remedies and sanctions

The consequences of breaching EU data protection law escalate dramatically under the GDPR, which sets the maximum fine for a single breach at the greater of €20 million, or four percent of annual worldwide turnover for the most serious breaches of the regulations

Transitional provisions

The GDPR was published on 4 May 2016, but enforcement does not begin until **25 May 2018**. The Directive, and the national laws that implement the Directive in Member States, continue to apply until the latter date

In addition to the changes in the articles in the GDPR there are the introduction of some key privacy principles, which will become your operating obligations, and therefore by extension the organisational culture. The 7 key Privacy Principles, introduced under the GDPR chapter on Data Protection where it discusses the objectives and requirements for technical and organisational measures, are fundamental to the GDPR are:

1. **Fair, lawful and transparent processing** - Personal data must be processed lawfully, fairly and in a **transparent manner** in relation to the data subject. (**Art.5(1)(a)**)

2. **The purpose limitation principle** - Personal data may only be collected for specified, explicit and legitimate purposes and must not be further processed in a manner that is incompatible with those purposes. **Art.5(1)(b)**

3. **Data minimisation** - Personal data must be adequate, relevant and **limited to what is necessary** in relation to the purposes for which those data are processed. **Art.5(1)(c)**

4. **Accuracy** - Personal data must be accurate and, where necessary, kept up to date. Every reasonable step must be taken to ensure that personal data that are inaccurate are either erased or rectified without delay. **Art.5(1)(d)**

5. **Data retention periods** - Personal data must be kept in a form that permits identification of data subjects for no longer than is necessary for the purposes for which the personal data are processed. **Art.5(1)(e)**

6. **Data security** - Personal data must be processed in a manner that ensures appropriate security of those data, including protection against unauthorised or unlawful processing and against accidental loss, destruction or damage, using appropriate technical or organisational measures. **Art.5(1)(f)**

7. **Accountability** - The controller is responsible for, **and must be able to demonstrate**, compliance with the Data Protection Principles. **Art.5(2)**

As you can probably see just from reading the Key Privacy Principles the onus has shifted firmly to the protection of the individual's rights and privacy. However it should also be clear that following the basic premise of the Privacy Principles will go a long way to mitigate many of the GDPR compliance threats or issues. For example, the concepts of data minimisation in collecting and holding only what you need and for a specific purpose is just good data governance.

Chapter II – GDPR Principles and New Articles

The aim of the GDPR is to protect all EU citizens' data privacy and to encourage the controllers and processors of personal data to show due diligence in carrying out their duties. Hence the GDPR is structured to prevent organizations needlessly collecting subjects personal data by enforcing accountability upon them for any data breaches in what is an increasingly cyber-hazardous world.

The GDPR is not radically different from its predecessor the DPD but it does strive to address the issues we now face in what is a vastly different world from 1995 the time the directive was established. Although the key principles of data privacy still hold true to the previous directive, several additions and expansions have been proposed to the regulatory policies.

What does this mean for you and your business?

Compliance with GDPR is necessary - it has far larger and sharper teeth that its predecessor the DPD, which had limited powers and scope, which led to some organizations treating it with distain. Instead the GDPR has real potential to inflict severe punishments for avoidance or non-compliance of the data privacy regulations of EU residents. However, it need not be looked upon solely as a threat or barrier to business instead it could actually make sound commercial sense, through providing competitive advantages, improve data governance and over-all cyber security, which will enhance customer confidence and as a result the organization's reputation.

GDPR is not a major impediment to organizations with sound data governance and data management already in place. Indeed many organizations that currently are in compliance with the existing DPD will only require making minor procedural updates to their working practices and data governance procedures. Companies that are proactive and move quickly on implementing GDPR are more likely to minimise the threat of penalties – as it is likely that being able to demonstrate willingness and intent to implement GDPR with all due diligence will go a long way in mitigating risk (the lawyers are already primed to respond to any customer complaints as a whole new revenue stream).

On the other hand for those organizations that have previously adopted a cavalier attitude towards the DPD, or have been genuinely ignorant of its very existence, had better watch out as the regulations applies to organizations of all sizes not just tech giants. One common fallacy is that GDPR only applies to large scale organizations, who are controllers, processors or both. However, the GDPR applies to organizations of all size that collects or process private identifiable information and that includes all those mobile app start-ups, those Internet of Things developers with an eye on innovation and blinded to the regulations and even those small Accountancy firms that provide a payroll service for SMBs. Therefore, companies of all size had better start to familiarize themselves with at least the new obligations and the increased regulatory landscape that come with the GDPR.

Increased Territorial Scope (extra-territorial applicability)

The change in the regulatory landscape is arguably one of the most significant changes that comes with the extended jurisdiction of the GDPR, as it applies to all companies processing the personal data of data subjects residing in the European Union, regardless of the company's location. Previously, territorial applicability of the directive was ambiguous and referred to data process 'in context of an establishment' and as a result of the directive being implemented differently across member states this led to variations in interpretation. As a result this topic has arisen in a number of high profile court cases. An aim of GPDR is to clarify its applicability and to make it very clear - it will apply to the processing of personal data by controllers and processors in the EU, regardless of whether the processing takes place in the EU or not. Furthermore, the GDPR will also apply to the processing of personal data of data subjects in the EU by a controller or processor not established in the EU, where the activities relate to: offering goods or services to EU citizens (irrespective of whether payment is required) and the monitoring of behaviour that takes place within the EU.

The scope of the regulatory powers in covering the offering of goods or services irrespective of payment and the monitoring of EU residents' internet behaviour is a clue to the type of business practices that the EU does not find acceptable. The GDPR is clear in its focus that the collection of personal data via monitoring or the provision of free applications or goods will require unambiguous consent and full compliance with GDPR. Additionally, non-EU businesses processing the data of EU citizens will also have to appoint a representative in the EU – this is to provide a regional point of contact.

Consequently for all organizations doing business in the EU and that includes the UK for the foreseeable future it would be highly advisable to check whether they are caught in the GDPR's extensive catchment area. Hence, the proactive actions that an organisation should take to prepare for the GDPR depends on whether the organisation comes under the EU GDPR the way to determine this is to consider that:

- An organisation established in the EU is subject to the GDPR,
- An organisation based outside the EU is subject to the GDPR if it either: (a) offers goods or services to EU data subjects (irrespective of charge); or (b) monitors the behaviour of EU data subjects.

Any organisation that is subject to the GDPR should review its obligations under the GDPR and take a risk-based approach, which we will cover later, in order to satisfying those obligations.

GDPR's expansion of Processor responsibility

GDPR directly regulates data processors for the first time as remember under the Directive the Data Processors had no obligations to the regulators and was only bound through their contractual obligations to their customers, the Controller. The Directive focused their attention solely on regulating the controllers the GDPR takes a very different perspective to the rules.

Under GDPR, that has all changed and processors might be in for a rude awakening as they will from May 25 2018 be required to comply with a number of specific obligations. The GDPR authorities will be enforcing the new processor regulations, which includes that they maintain adequate documentation, comply with rules on international data transfers, carry out routine data protection impact assessments, implement appropriate technical and organisational measures (security standards), appoint a data protection officer and cooperate with national supervisory authorities. These are in addition to the requirement for controllers to ensure that when appointing a processor, a written data processing agreement (contract) is put in place meeting the requirements of GDPR.

In addition as Processors are no longer free from regulation or liability under GDPR they will be directly liable to sanctions if they fail to meet these criteria and may also face private claims by individuals for compensation. Consequently there is a significant risk that a non-European Processor may not wish to agree to the terms in a Controller contract necessary for GDPR compliance in providing a service. Therefore the Controller should take early steps to ensure the continuity of service provided by their existing service providers in processing their data under GDPR compliant contracts.

From a practical point of view GDPR changes the risk profile for those service suppliers processing personal data (processors) on behalf of their customers (controllers). Processors now face the threat of revenue based fines and private claims by individuals for failing to comply with GDPR and protect their personal data. Attempting to claim ignorance and passing the buck back onto the controller won't work anymore; as the DPA can fine both of them. Suppliers of data processing services therefore will need to take responsibility for compliance and assess their own obligation and readiness for compliance with GDPR. In many cases this will require a full review and overhaul of current operational practices and especially of contracting arrangements to ensure better compliance on a per controller/contract basis. The increased compliance burden and risk can be mitigated through Data Impact and Privacy Assessments but it will still require a careful review of individual Controller contracts.

2. Processors will need to review each contract with their customers the controllers and decide for each type of processing undertaken whether they are acting solely as a processor or if their processing arrangements could allow them to be mistaken for a data controller or a joint controller, thereby attracting the full burden of GDPR.

3. Customers (as controllers) face similar challenges as they are responsible for vetting the processor and the contracts for service. Supply chains will need to be reviewed and assessed to determine current compliance with GDPR. Privacy impact assessments will need to be carried out although Processors may already have completed and published a PIA for their services. In some cases supervisory authorities may need to be consulted for advice to delineate the fine line between Controller and Processor. In many cases contracts are likely to need to be overhauled to meet the new requirements of GDPR. These negotiations will not be straightforward given the increased risk and compliance burden for suppliers. Indeed the fear is that some non-European Processors or service providers may not want to conform to the GDPR. As compliance will not only be onerous but costly and also time consuming. However to ensure GDPR complaint contracts are in place before spring 2018 it would be sensible to start the renegotiation exercise sooner rather than later, particularly as suppliers are likely to take a more inflexible view over time as standard positions are developed.

4. However, it is not all bad news accompanying every major challenge come an opportunity and with the burdens of GDPR comes the opportunities for Processors to offer GDPR "compliance as a

service" solutions. By providing a PaaS to GDPR for compliance for the SMEs market such as a secure cloud solutions, the Processors can relieve the customers' of the heavy lifting of compliance. Customers though will need to review these carefully to ensure they dovetail to their own compliance strategy.

Therefore in summary organisations that act as processors, or act as controllers that engage processors, should carefully review the requirements associated with appointing processors. In addition, each organisation that acts as a processor should:

- identify the data processing activities for which it is a contracted processor;
- ensure that it understands its responsibilities and legal obligations as a processor under the GDPR; and
- ensure that it has appropriate technical and organizational measures and processes in place for identifying, reviewing and promptly reporting data breaches to the relevant controller.

GDPR's expanded concept of consent

The GDPR expands on the requirement of the DPD by the instruction that Data Controllers must receive explicit consent from EU residents in order for them to lawfully process their personal data or monitor their behaviour.
The question of whether a data subject has unambiguously or in certain scenario explicitly given their consent for an organization to monitor their behaviour or collect their personal data is paramount in the GDPR. The issue being that over the last decade a common business model of providing free services in exchange for personal data – in a kind of unofficial barter arrangement. However, often the barter is not clear, let alone documented and agreed, often to the extent that the user of the service may not even know that their private data is being collected. This situation arises for a number of reasons

sometimes it is because the *agreement* is based on a common belief or as a result of the agreement being hidden within pages of indecipherable legalese within the Terms and Condition of use or in the Privacy Policy. Therefore in order to ensure that EU resident's privacy is being respected and they are protected from some dubious practices to obtain their consent the GDPR focuses firmly upon the concept of unambiguous consent.

As a result the condition for obtaining consent has been strengthened, and companies will now have to request for consent and it must be given in an intelligible and easily readable form, with the specific purpose for data processing highlighted to the user and then attached to that consent. What that means is that the consent an individual gives is only for the purpose stated it is not an umbrella agreement so for each additional but different purpose, additional consent must be sought. Further, the user's consent is specific to the named organization for that purpose only and cannot be assumed for any alternative purpose or passed on to a third party. Consent must be clear and distinguishable from other matters and provided in an intelligible and easily accessible form, using clear and plain language.

Furthermore, consent must be unambiguous; therefore it requires affirmative action such as the individual signing a statement or a mechanism to opt-in to a service. Non-action, silence or passive agreement are not considered as acceptable consent neither are pre-selected tick boxes nor opt-out mechanisms that place the onus on the individual to withhold their consent.

Very importantly it must be as easy for the user to withdraw their consent as it is to give it.

Consent is a tricky and complex principle as there is a minimum requirement for unambiguous consent as the standard but explicit consent is the minimum standard for obtaining consent for data in special categories which we will discuss later. In summary as a quick checklist the UK's Information Commission Office (ICO) provides these guidelines:

- The GDPR sets a high standard for consent.

- Doing consent well should put individuals in control, build customer trust and engagement, and enhance your reputation.

- Check your consent practices and your existing consents. Refresh consents if they don't meet the GDPR standard.

- Consent means offering individuals genuine choice and control

- Consent requires a positive opt-in. Don't use pre-ticked boxes or any other method of consent by default

- Explicit consent requires a very clear and specific statement of consent.

- Keep your consent requests separate from other terms and conditions.

- Be specific and granular. Vague or blanket consent is not enough.

- Be clear and concise.

- Name any third parties who will rely on the consent.

- Make it easy for people to withdraw consent and tell them how.

- Keep evidence of consent – who, when, how, and what you told people.

Keep consent under review, and refresh it if anything changes.

- Avoid making consent a precondition of a service.

- Public authorities and employers will find using consent difficult.

- Remember – you don't always need consent. If consent is too difficult, look at whether another lawful basis is more appropriate.

Data Subject Rights

The GDPR focuses on individual rights, and on transparency and accountability principles which underpin the GDPR. As a result, the overwhelming aim of the regulation is to put individuals and their rights as paramount. Hence, the GDPR extends and strengthens some existing rights which individuals can exercise against controllers, as well as introducing a number of new rights. However the GDPR does not bestow absolute rights there will be restrictions and exceptions and data subjects should have their rights and limitations clearly explained to them. Similarly, Controllers will need to consider all aspects of their processing activities in light of the rights afforded to individuals.

Member State laws still trump GDPR as can be demonstrated for example in the case of the Investigative Powers Act in the UK, which requires service providers to collect and store all user communications originating on their networks. This places service providers in a difficult position as they are caught between the privacy rights of their users, the GDPR regulations and the Laws of the State. This is where having robust and mature data governance strategy and data management mechanisms will enable Controllers to ultimately be in a position to demonstrate compliance not only when individuals seek to exercise those rights, but with their overall obligations under the GDPR and State Law.

Breach Notification

Another weak area of the DPD was the latitude that Controllers and Processors had when notifying the authorities and data subjects of potential breaches of confidentiality or integrity. Indeed there have been some well publicized incidents where some organizations based out with the EU but processing large amounts of EU residents personal data have failed to disclose breaches and the potential disclosure of personal data, including passwords, for over two years. Disclosure of data breaches is problematic because it is not always clear if a breach has indeed occurred or to what extent that private data may have become disclosed to or compromised by a third party.

Due to the often ambiguous nature of a breach organizations are loath to notify an authority until they have carried out their investigations and ascertained the root cause and mitigated any vulnerability. However this can lead to unacceptable delays as the longer it goes without anyone complaining then the more difficult it becomes to go public and the temptation to stay silent hence the two year example given previously.

Consequently, to address this obvious shortcoming breach notification will become mandatory in all member states where a data breach is likely to "result in a risk for the rights and freedoms of individuals". Under GDPR, notification must be done within 72 hours of first having become aware of the breach. Data processors will also be required to notify their customers, the controllers, "without undue delay" after first becoming aware of a data breach.

Now, this is 72 hours from when you first become aware of the breach so that is an onerous schedule, which will require efficient breach detection, security breach procedures and notification processes to be in place for this procedure to work efficiently – if at all.

Right to Access

'Privacy is dead' or 'Privacy is irrelevant in the internet age' are statements that are commonly touted on social media and by the owners or CEOs of the technology giants that dominate social media and internet search, browsing and communications. The architects of the GDPR in their wisdom have taken a different approach in defending the fundamental rights of the individual to privacy.

One of the catalysts for defending the rights of the individual's privacy was a growing aversion to the subterfuge and pervasive use of insidious techniques implemented by the tech giants to harvest users' person data with or without their consent. It was this arrogance and subterfuge that the tech giants defended by claiming that their subscribers received services for free that would otherwise cost a considerable sum. Therefore it was a kind of barter and exchange of goods, quality services for personal data, and this is so deeply ingrained into the psychology of the tech giants that they feel aggrieved when a subscriber has the audacity to use an ad-blocker or the temerity to refuse third party site cookies.

To be fair the tech giants do supply a quality service to their subscribers but they have often been less than transparent regards the purpose of collecting individuals (subscribers and non-subscribers) personal data or indeed their overall business model. Where the tech giants fell afoul of the EU regulators was when they started to monitor not only their own subscribers or visitors to their sites, their web real estate, but even non-subscribers who happened to visit a third party website on which the tech giants had placed a web widget. This was a significant ethical departure from the barter model or lame excuse because now they were harvesting personal web data via third party cookies from even non-subscribers to their service. Indeed now they were misappropriating the personal data of many EU residents that did not subscribe to their services but nonetheless where subjected to having their behaviour monitored.

A classic example of this monitoring by subterfuge was Facebook v.EU Belgian DPA. The issue revolved around Facebook's use of its social plug-in such as the "Like" button, which they had been placing on more than 13 million third party websites including even Public Health and Government websites. Although Facebook are by no means the only ones using this dubious practice it was them that came into conflict originally with the Belgium DPA.

What riled the EU DPA was that when a user visits a third-party site that carries one of Facebook's social plug-ins, the code detects and sends the tracking cookies information back to Facebook - even if the user does not interact with the Like button, Facebook Login or other extension on the third party site. Just browsing to a Public Health site or a government information web page may be sufficient for them to be tracked as they go about their future online activity.

EU privacy law states that prior consent must be given before issuing a cookie or performing tracking, unless it is necessary for either the networking required to connect to the service ("criterion A") or to deliver a service specifically requested by the user ("criterion B").

The same law requires websites to notify users on their first visit to a site that it uses cookies, requesting consent to do so. Currently many website comply with this regulation but their mechanisms for approval are passive, and consent is implied through the individual continuing to view or interact with the website, this will no longer be acceptable under GDPR as affirmative action will be required.

This is just one example of why there is a requirement for GDPR to tighten up on the amount of data subject's personal data that is harvested with or without their unambiguous consent.

As a result the GDPR has strengthened the hand of the individual in forcing organizations to surrender all personal data held that has been collected – law enforcement and Intelligence Service being exceptions - with or without a individual's consent. Hence, the GDPR ensures that an individual has continuing but stronger rights under the regulation to establish whether a controller processes information relating to him / her, and to access and obtain a copy of that data and certain additional information in relation to the processing, such as its purposes, the categories of data, the existence of any third party, and the recipients of the data sharing.

There are also some additional rights such as the rights to erasure and objection. In response several of the tech giants have made such information available voluntarily and it surprises many subscribers to see the amount of data the web giants are capturing, storing and processing about them.

Currently, data access is a right but organization for many reasons place hurdles in the way as it is not convenient – the harsh reality being that as often as not the whereabouts of a customer's data may not be known. GDPR enhances the exercise by an individual of his / her access rights but the right of access is not an absolute right and cannot prejudice the rights and freedoms of other individuals.

Therefore, it is important to realize that although individuals have enhanced powers over the rights of access to their personal data it must not infringe upon the rights of others to maintain their right of privacy.

As a result under GDPR one part of the expanded rights of data subjects is the right for data subjects to obtain from the data controller confirmation as to whether or not personal data concerning them is being processed, where and for what purpose, to whom it may be disclosed to and importantly they may ask for copies of all personal data that the Controller hold regards them.

Currently under the DPD, a subject can through a Subject Access Request (SAR) submit a request for information to a Data Controller for example an employee could submit to an employer a request for information;

- whether it processes his personal data;
- what personal data the employer holds, the sources of such data, the purposes for which it is being processed and to whom it is disclosed; and
- for copies of the personal data held.

The GDPR expands on some of the rights under the DPD such as the subject can now request for information regarding;

    (i) the retention period for the personal data processed;
    (ii) information on any automated decision-making or profiling, if relevant, the logic involved and

the consequences of such processing for the individual; and (iii) the existence of the rights to rectify or delete the personal data concerning him, or to restrict or object to the processing of his personal data.

Furthermore, the controller under GDPR shall now have to provide a copy of the personal data, free of charge, in an electronic format within one month. This change is a dramatic shift towards data transparency and empowerment of data subjects as previously organizations could charge for the service and organizations were comforted by the fact that when a fee is charged many requestors abandoned their query. In addition they could delay the process and take up to six weeks or longer depending on the amount of questions asked thereby making the whole procedure less attractive to the inquirer.

There are allowances made for the complexity of the SAR, which can extend the period the Controller has in order to respond. However 'complexity' is not clearly defined and is likely to be fact and context dependent. The GDPR suggests that where the controller processes a large quantity of information about the subject, for example a Public Health site, the Controller should ask the requestor to "specify the information or processing activities to which the request relates". This is intended to help the Controller narrow their search and to reduce the complexity of searching and compiling related and relevant information. The GDPR also intends to encourage the subject to narrow down their requests as more precise requests – rather than fishing for information - limit the Controller's ability to show complexity – after all the onus is still on the Controller to demonstrate complexity.

A similar position is taken with regards Controllers' complaints that most SARs are excessive or unfounded. The GDPR again places the burden upon the Controller to demonstrate that the SAR would require disproportional effort in order to comply. An example of this could be an employee's request to an employer that would require trawling through thousands of documents and emails to discover any traces of employee personal data and the employer could consider this to be excessive. Similarly, if an employer diligently complies with the guidance of the GDPR and processes personal data transparently and fairly then it is likely that an employee SAR that is a non-specific broad request for any personal identifiable information, which amounts to no more than a fishing exercise, would be considered to be unfounded.

However, as the GDPR is designed to increase and improve data subjects' rights, the burden will be on the employer to demonstrate that a request is 'excessive' or 'unfounded'.

Right to be Forgotten

The 'Right to be Forgotten' is arguably one of the most famous or notorious victories for the EU against the Internet-sized tech giants as it set a precedent for the right to remove out-dated or personal data where an individual no longer provided consent.

During the test case which involved Google v. Spain, the European Court of Justice ruled that the European citizens have a right to request that commercial search firms, such as Google, that gather personal information for profit should remove links to private information when asked, provided the information is no longer relevant. However what was interesting is that the ECJ court did not say that publishers, the main stream media such as newspaper's online editions or data archives should remove articles or references. Indeed had Google determined that they were indeed a publisher they could have sidestepped this ruling very neatly however it seems Google doesn't wish to be categorised as a publisher so had to accept the ruling.

The Google v. Spain case sent shockwaves around the world especially amongst the internet search organizations as the European Court of Justice found that the fundamental right to privacy is greater than the economic interest of the commercial firm and, in some circumstances, the public interest in access to information. Furthermore, it was the decision of the European Court to affirm the judgment of the Spanish Data Protection Agency which upheld press freedoms and rejected a request to have the article concerning personal bankruptcy removed from the web site of the press organization. As a result the decision was that the 'right to be forgotten' applied only to commercial organizations such as search providers and direct marketers but not to media or publishing organizations that required maintaining a history of events.

The 'Right to be Forgotten' clause, which is also known as Data Erasure, is the right to be forgotten, which entitles the data subject to have the data controller erase his/her personal data, and to cease further dissemination of the data, and cease the propagation to third parties and potentially the requirement to urge third parties to halt processing of the previously disseminated data. The conditions for erasure, as outlined in article 17 of the GDPR, include the data no longer being relevant to original purposes for processing, or a data subjects withdrawing consent.

What this means in practice is that a Controller which receives a request under the 'right to be forgotten' clause may be where possible required to not only delete any personal data they hold on the individual but also to pursue any third parties they have shared the data with to ensure that they too delete the data. This additional burden is another enticing reason for Controllers to embrace the principle of data minimization, purpose and transparency.

However, the Right to be Forgotten clause is not an absolute right by any means and it should also be noted that this right requires controllers to compare the subjects' rights to "the public interest in the availability of the data" when considering such requests.

Consequently, Google and the other Tech giants must now evaluate millions of URLs that have been requested to be removed. The ultimate decision must be made by a human "because the variables, including public interest claims, needs to be handled on a case-by-case basis". However, although the letter of the law may be adhered to the sprit may still be weak as internet users can still find the so termed forgotten information somewhat easily through using non-European Google search engines.

An interesting aside regards the Right to be Forgotten clause, is that out of all the requests that Google processed up until May 2015 they found that around 95% were from citizens out to protect personal and private information – and not criminals, politicians and public figures.

As is demonstrated by the Google vs. Spain case the right to have personal data rectified, blocked or erased already exists under existing data protection rules. However, enforcing those rights involves a relatively high threshold for individuals, and requires a demonstration that the data controller has contravened data protection principles. Partly as a result of the Google vs. Spain decision by the Court of Justice of the European Union, however, there has been much more emphasis on the right of erasure or "the right to be forgotten", and this focus is reflected in the provisions of the GDPR.

Therefore under the GDPR, every individual has the right to have his / her data erased, or the "right to be forgotten", in circumstances where:

- the data is no longer necessary for the purpose for which they were collected;
- processing is based on consent, but the individual has withdrawn consent and there is no other legal ground for continued processing available to the controller;
- an individual has exercised his / her right to object, and there is no overriding legitimate interest on which the controller can continue to legitimise its processing;
- the data is unlawfully processed;
- the erasure is required by a law applicable to the controller; or
- the data was collected in connection with the offer of information society services to a child.

The Right to be Forgotten clause however is not an absolute right, and a controller will be in a position to continue processing the data on the basis of freedom of expression and information, where the controller is required to comply with the legal obligation which requires processing (bearing in mind that this has to arise under EU or member state laws), or if the processing is required to establish, exercise or defend legal claims.

Right to Object

As with the right to be forgotten, the right to object to processing personal data already exists in connection with for example, direct marketing. There is also the right to object where the processing being performed is based on a legitimate purpose of the controller; however an individual has the right to object to the processing for specified purposes or in a specified manner on the ground that, for specified reasons, it causes or is likely to cause unwarranted substantial damage or distress.

There some are some specific types of processing that subjects can object:
- Direct marketing;
- Processing based on legitimate interests or performance of a task in the public interest/exercise of official authority; and
- Processing for research or statistical purposes.

However it should be noted that only the right to object to direct marketing is absolute (i.e. there is no need for the subject to demonstrate any grounds for objecting, and there are no exemptions which allow processing to continue).

Moreover there are obligations to notify individuals of these rights at an early stage - clearly and separately from other information.

Under the GDPR, the existing right to object to processing continues, along with some clarifications and expansion. As is currently the case, an individual has the right to object to direct marketing at any time, and in that event, the controller must stop using the information for marketing purposes. However, an individual can also object where:

- retaining the data is no longer necessary for the purposes for which collected;
- Consent has been withdrawn and there is no other legitimate ground for processing;
- processing is based on a public interest or a legitimate interest of the controller, in which case, unless there is overriding legitimate interests, the controller must cease the processing. In this regard, there is no longer any reference to their being "unwarranted substantial damage or distress to the data subject", and instead, controllers must take into account "grounds relating to the data subjects particular situation", which is a broader concept;
- the data has been unlawfully processed;
- erasure is required under a legal obligation to which the controller is subject under EU or member state law; or
- the data was collected in the context of the provision of information society services to a child.

For organizations to address the concerns of the Right to Object they should consider introducing audit data protection notices and policies to ensure that individuals are told about their right to object, clearly and separately, at the point of 'first communication'.

For web based or online services, organizations must ensure that there is an automated way for this to be effected for example a link or widget on the site that is easily accessible; and for marketers they should review marketing suppression lists and processes (including those operated on behalf of your organisation by partners and service providers) to ensure they are capable of operating in compliance with the GDPR.

Data Portability

Of course not all clauses are impediments to business with GDPR, for example the case of data portability does enable small businesses and start-ups to entice customers away from the long established internet companies who may be trying to lock in their customers. For example to change mobile phone or email provider is now relatively straightforward as you can port your private data such as number, address books, emails, and history etc along with you to the new service provider. Hence, GDPR aims to build upon data subjects rights to freedom of movement of their personal data whether that is to a personal device or to another service provider.

In addition, the GDPR introduces the concepts of data portability as a new right, which allows individuals to obtain and, importantly, reuse their personal data from the incumbent provider. In practice a data subject can either obtain the data him / herself and, in turn, provide it to a third party or require the incumbent data controller to transfer the personal data directly to a third party on their behalf.

The point of the data transfer clause is to ensure that the GDPR introduces the concept of data portability - the right for a data subject to receive and then transport their personal data, which concerns them. Further, they can expect to receive their personal data which they have previously provided in a '*commonly used and machine readable format*' and they will have the right to transmit that data to another controller without additional fees being payable for the service or experience any further business restrictions.

The right to data portability is a new right under GDPR, which the Working Party Article 29 emphasises, is intended to give data subjects more control over their personal data, especially to reuse and manage it, or to switch between service providers. Under the GDPR, data subjects:

"...have the right to receive the personal data concerning him or her, which he or she has provided to a controller, in a structured, commonly used and machine-readable format and have the right to transmit those data to another controller without hindrance from the controller to which the data have been provided..."

A number of key areas are clarified by the guidelines, including: when does the right apply and to what data; what practical measures can be used to comply with the right; and how does it relate to other data subject rights.

For example the GDPR sets out to clarify when the right to data portability will apply and to what data. This was not always clear under the DPD but now according to the guidelines we see that *"the GDPR does not establish a general right of data portability"*.

To clarify and be specific, the right to data portability only applies to information being processed with the data subject's consent or pursuant to a contract. This means that personal data which is processed under one of the other permitted conditions of processing – for example, because it is necessary for the data controller's legitimate interests – would not be covered.

In addition and importantly, the GDPR makes a distinction between personal obtained through, data generated by and collected from the activities of data subjects, which would be covered by the data portability right, versus information or knowledge which the Controller has inferred or derived from the customer provided data, which would not be in scope. So, for example, data exclusively generated by the data controller through its own algorithms, such as a user profile, inferred customer preferences or sales lead history may not be covered. This also extends to cover the rights of data controllers and other parties in protecting their own trade secrets and other intellectual property. Hence, the information covered by the right to data portability must also be considered in light of the Controller's rights to protect their privacy but according to the WP29 *"cannot, however, in and of itself serve as the basis for a refusal to answer the portability request"*.

For Controllers to be able to comply with the rights of data portability there are some practical measures that can be taken to ensure compliance. Hence in order to comply with the right to data portability it is envisaged that data controllers will need to implement some technical tools in order to handle the requirements of the rights. These tools will include at a minimum a mechanism or process for acknowledging receipt of requests, ascertaining the identity of the data subject and responding to the requests without undue delay – something which WP29 anticipates should be technically possible for controllers operating information society services to do in a very short-time period. This should be required a prerequisite as it is imperative that the Controller demonstrates that they are handling the requests diligently.

Note: The WP29 and GDPR often refer to Information Society Services, which can be defined under law as; *any service normally provided for remuneration, at a distance, by means of electronic equipment for the processing (including digital compression) and storage of data, and at the individual request of a recipient of a service.*

Additional technical measures that may be required for providing and delivering the information can include mechanisms or processes that allow data subjects to download their personal data directly from the controller's website or to directly transmit the data to another data controller, for example, by way of an API or connector, and that the format must support re-use and ensure the data will be interpretable.

Another method may be to use the services of a trusted third party which could be used as a store for personal data to which the data subject then grants access.

The question often arises as to how the right to data portability will relate to other data subject rights and the GDPR and WP29 guidelines confirm that the right to data portability does not affect a data subject's ability to exercise his/her other rights. For example, it does not automatically trigger the deletion of data from a controller's systems and it should not stop a data subject from continuing to use and benefit from other services provided by the data controller. As a result the GDPR makes provision for a subject to have a right to receive personal data ("in a structured, commonly used and machine-readable format") processed by a data controller, and to store it for further personal use on a private device, without transferring it to another data controller. This right offers an easy way for the data subjects to manage their personal data themselves.

Privacy by Design

Privacy by design, is one of those phrases that crop up over a vast array of disciplines, it has as a concept existed across all industry design and best practices for many years now, but it is only just becoming part of a legal requirement with the GDPR.

Why the internet has been so slow to protect individuals privacy can only be surmised to be due to the different cultural expectations and demands for personal data privacy.
For example in the EU personal privacy is considered to be a basic human right whereas in the United States, which is arguably the closest nation that shares most of the EU's values, personal data privacy is unfortunately not one of them. Hence, all the political issues pertaining to the lawful transportation of personal data across the Atlantic.

In the EU however the rights of residents to data privacy is enshrined under EU Human Rights law and so GDPR has at its core, the concept of Privacy by Design and Privacy by Default.
In essence, Privacy by Design is not some fancy buzz-words it is a fundamental design paradigm, which calls for the inclusion of data protection from the onset of the designing of systems, rather than an addition.

More specifically - *'The controller shall...implement appropriate technical and organisational measures...in an effective way... in order to meet the requirements of this Regulation and protect the rights of data subjects'.*

Within the text of Article 23 of GDPR the article calls for Controllers to hold and process only the data absolutely necessary for the completion of its duties (the concept of data minimisation), and this also applies to restricting the access to personal data to only those needing to perform the actual storage and processing.
In addition, within the GDPR articles there is an existing right not to be subjected to processing which is wholly automated and which may well produce effects that have far reaching ramifications, legal or

otherwise. As a result the GDPR limits and restricts the use of wholly automated processing which can significantly affect an individual, especially those which are intended to evaluate certain personal matters, such as creditworthiness or performance at work, unless one of a limited number of exemptions applies.

A major principle that supports the purpose of the GDPR is that EU residents as data subjects will always continue to have the right not to be subject to decisions based solely on automated processing. Interestingly, the GDPR specifically references profiling, which is defined as;

"any form of automated process to evaluate certain personal aspects relating to a natural person, in particular to analyse or predict aspects concerning performance at work, economic situation, health, personal preferences, interests, reliability, behaviour, location or movements".

(Note: This principle sets GDPR on a huge collision course with the current business appetite for Artificial Intelligence and Machine Learning algorithms and the systems where the technology and algorithms will be embedded.)

The exceptions to automated decision making are more narrowly drawn than under current DPD rules. Whereas previously under the provisions in the DPD, such processing was permitted in the course of considering whether to enter into a contract, or with a view to entering into a contract or for the performance of a contract, under the GDPR, automated processing will only be permitted, in the context of a contract, where it is a "contractual necessity".

In addition, where a controller seeks to rely on consent, it must be explicit consent. Explicit consent is a higher standard to unambiguous consent so the barriers to obtaining it are far higher. In both cases of consent, the controller is obliged to implement a minimum set of suitable safeguards, so "at least" the right to obtain human intervention, to express views and to contest the decision should be built into the process.

Like we noted earlier this has interesting potential for conflict with the pervasive entry into the technology marketplace of AI and Machine Learning algorithms in Finance (FinTech), Insurance and Retail to name just a few. So it will be intriguing how GDPR manages to co-exist with these highly attractive and soon to be state-of-the-art technologies.

Transparency

The concept of Transparency is one of the fundamental pillars that underpin the existing European data protection framework. The GDPR already places extensive and in some cases specific obligations on organisations to be fair, open and honest about the ways that they use information about EU residents and individual's private data. Transparency relates to the requirement that organisations be fair, open and truthful with subjects as to the what, why, who, where and how in relation to the processing of their private data.

Indeed by respecting those core principles in accord with a diligent data governance strategy will go a considerable way to success on the quest for compliance to the GDPR.

What transparency means in practice is that before processing any EU residents personal data an organization must first ensure that the data subjects are clearly and unambiguously told what information will be processed, why and for what specific purpose, who will process their personal data and where, and how they can exercise their rights should they object.

The existing DPD requirements for a Controller to ask a subject to provide private data information is that they must clearly inform them and:
- Provide the identity of the data controller (or any representative)
- The purposes for which the data is being collected and processed
- Any further information needed to ensure that the data is processed

fairly

However, importantly the GDPR expands that list to cover the following additional information for the lawful process of private data:

- The specific "legitimate purposes" of the controller, where the processing in based on this legal ground.
- The period for which the personal data will be stored.
- The different rights available to individuals established by law.
- The right to complain to a data protection authority and the contact details of the authority.
- Whether the personal data will be transferred internationally.
- Whether the provision of personal data is obligatory or voluntary (when collected directly from individuals).
- The source of the data (when collected from third parties).

Unfortunately, it probably would not require a GAP analysis to establish the vast chasm between the current privacy practices of contemporary online and tech organizations and the GDPR requirements. To compound the issue is the expectation that any information relating to the processing of personal information must use clear and plain language which is tailored to the relevant audience and must also be easily accessible, it is clear that most organizations will fail due to having a diametrically skewed position on informing the user of their intentions let alone the user's rights.
Consequently it is glaringly obvious that most organisations will require a full scale review of their Terms and Conditions, Privacy Statements, Contact Centre scripts and user engagement policies amongst many other engagement collateral touch-points in order to meet the expanded transparency requirements.

Currently it is the nonchalant belief held by organizations that nobody bothers to read the T&C let alone the privacy policies. Hence, the reason that they politically hide anything contentious deep within the verbose legalese of these mock legal documents. Even if the data subject shows admirable endeavour and should wish to wade through pages of legalese the verbose and deliberately slumber inducing text will soon put them off. However, should they persevere then only the best legal minds will be able to comprehend the legalese – if indeed that is even possible. However with the enforcement of GDPR the organisations using these dubious tactics are gambling against the possibility of fines of up to €20,000,000, or up to 4% of annual worldwide turnover whichever is the highest. The risk of such fines alone should enlighten the board of directors and senior executives for the need of a new more acceptable approach to privacy and transparency. Indeed perhaps the hope is that the size of the penalties should be incentive enough to get Boards to enforce an urgent review of the organizational culture, policies and procedures.

Of course the opposite may well be true, and this is where an organization does spell out frankly and in all its glorious but shameful detail the exact shenanigans of the organizations Privacy Policy. The point being that as it is unlikely that anyone will ever read the Terms and Conditions or the Privacy Policy articles it is actually safe enough to be brutally honest. For example one web organization that pertains to supply answers to all sorts of scientific, technical and philosophical questions has a brutal privacy policy whereby the company frankly states that not only will they ignore any wish that an individual may state not to be tracked, the request will be ignored and they will track you anyway using all sorts of persistent cookies and also actively use Clear Gifs technology to determine if a subscriber has opened an email from them as well as sell on the subjects personal details and online behaviour with or without the individual's consent.

Unfortunately, they are not the only ones using such odious tactics as it appears that many web service organizations ignore a browser setting for 'Do not track' as it is simply a browser request. Consequently, many web based tech companies have a considerable way to go in meeting EU standards of transparency and the principle of fair, open and honest handling of an individual's personal data let alone their right to privacy and these organisations could be in for a major shock

Data Protection Officers

Arguably the most contentious issue with regards the GDPR is the concept of organizations having to hire a Data Protection Officer. In many Q&A sessions with organisations the prime subject of interest for organizations is the clarification of the need for or the role of the Date Protection Officer.

In short according to the GDPR, a DPO is required by controllers and processors in only three specific cases:

- where the processing is carried out by a public authority or body;
- where the core activities of the controller or the processor consist of processing operations, which require regular and systematic monitoring of data subjects on a large scale; or
- where the core activities of the controller or the processor consist of processing on a large scale of special categories of data, or personal data relating to criminal convictions and offences.

The working party guidelines clarify the criteria and terminology used in the GDPR:

'Core activities' are described as the key operations necessary to achieve the controller's or processor's goals. Necessary support functions such standard IT support are usually considered ancillary functions rather than the core activity.

However, whether a processing activity is carried out on a 'large scale' is not so easily quantified and will depend on a number of factors; including the number of data subjects concerned, the volume of data and/or the range of data items being processed, the duration or permanence of the processing, and the geographical extent of the processing.

'Regular and system monitoring' is not confined to the online environment and online tracking. Other examples include: the operation of a telecommunications network; profiling and scoring for the purposes of risk assessment; location tracking; fitness and health data via wearable devices; and connected IoT devices. Therefore this interpretation can open up the potential field of what may be considered to be personal data to a much broader category of data and devices.

Consequently, unless it is obvious that an organisation does not require a DPO, the organisation should still document the internal analysis carried out to determine whether one is required – again this is to demonstrate due diligence in preparation for GDPR.

If the organization comes to the executive decision that a DPO is not mandatory, then an organisation may decide to designate a DPO on a part time voluntary basis. However, that may not be such an attractive solution when you consider that should they do so, then the same requirements under Articles 37 to 39 of the GDPR will apply to his or her designation, position and tasks as if the designation had been mandatory.

An alternative is to appoint a third party as DPO for the organization as a DPO can perform their role for one or more organizations so hiring the services of a specialist DPO may be a more attractive solution for some organizations. Beware however as the DPO is a protected position so will be protected to some extent regarding unfair termination of a service contract this is also true of an employee as they too will become protected from termination due to their role as DPO.

In addition, caution should be exercised with the voluntary appointment of a DPO as it should not be confused with staff or outside consultants who have tasks relating to the protection of personal data (but who are not given the title or role of DPO).

What is the role of a DPO?

The DPO must be involved, from the earliest stage possible, in all issues relating to the protection of personal data. Appropriately informing the DPO should be a standard procedure within the organisation's governance. That means that they should be: invited to participate regularly in meetings of senior and middle management; present where decisions with data protection implications are taken; and promptly consulted once a data breach or other incident has occurred. According to the WP29, the DPO will *"play a key role in fostering a data protection culture within the organisation"*.

The DPO's Tasks

A DPO must be *"easily accessible from each establishment"*. That means that a group of undertakings can appoint a single DPO, as long as he or she is personally available to efficiently communicate with data subjects, supervisory authorities and internally within the organisation (including in the language or languages of the supervisory authorities or data subjects concerned). A single DPO must be able to perform their tasks efficiently despite being responsible for several undertakings.

A DPO must have the necessary skills and expertise, which should be determined according to the data processing activities carried out and the protection required for the personal data being processed. An in-depth understanding of the GDPR is essential, and knowledge of the business sector and of the organisation is useful.

A DPO can be appointed on a part-time basis, alongside other duties; provided that those other duties do not give rise to conflicts of interest and as long as the DPO is given sufficient time to fulfil their duties as a DPO.

An external DPO or even a DPO team may be appointed, provided that the DPO must be able to fulfil its / their tasks, they must be independent and they must be afforded sufficient protection (for example, from unfair termination of a service contract).

According to the GDPR Article regarding the DPO, who can be a staff member or contractor, they shall be designated on the basis of professional qualities and, in particular, expert knowledge of data protection law and practices and the ability to fulfil the tasks referred to in the GDPR Articles. These are more specifically:

- to inform and advise the controller or the processor and the employees who are
processing personal data of their obligations pursuant to this Regulation;
- to monitor compliance with this Regulation, including the assignment of responsibilities, awareness- raising and training of staff involved in the processing operations, and the related audits;
- to provide advice where requested as regards the data protection impact assessment and monitor its performance pursuant to Article 35;
- to cooperate with the supervisory authority (the ICO in the UK);
- to act as the contact point for the supervisory authority on issues related to the processing of personal data

Qualities required of a DPO

The GDPR Article 29 Working Party Guidance states:

"Although Article 37 does not specify the professional qualities that should be considered when designating the DPO, it is a relevant element that DPOs should have expertise in national and European data protection laws and practices and an in depth understanding of the GDPR. It is also helpful if the supervisory authorities promote adequate and regular training for DPOs."

This implies that the necessary level of expert knowledge should be determined according to the data processing operations carried out and the protection required for the personal data being processed. For example, where a data processing activity is particularly complex, or where a large amount of sensitive data is involved, the DPO may need a higher level of specific subject matter expertise and perhaps addition SME support. Generally, the necessary skills and expertise include:

- expertise in national and European data protection laws and practices including an in depth
- understanding of the GDPR
- understanding of the processing operations carried out
- understanding of information technologies and data security
- knowledge of the business sector and the organisation
- ability to promote a data protection culture within the organisation

The DPO must be allowed to perform tasks in an independent manner and should not receive any instructions regarding the exercise of their tasks. She/he reports to the highest management level in the organisation and cannot be dismissed or penalised for doing their job.

Article 38(2) of GDPR requires the organisation to support its DPO by "providing resources necessary to carry out [their] tasks and access to personal data and processing operations, and to maintain his or her expert knowledge." The A29 Guidance says that, depending on the nature of the processing operations and the activities and size of the organisation, the following resources should be provided to the DPO:

- Active support of the DPO's function by senior management
- Sufficient time to for DPOs to fulfil their duties
- Adequate support in terms of financial resources, infrastructure (premises, facilities, equipment) and staff where appropriate
- Official communication of the designation of the DPO to all staff
- Access to other services within the organisation so that DPOs can receive essential support, input or information from those other services
- Continuous training

The DPO will be at the heart of the data protection framework for many organisations, facilitating compliance with the provisions of the

GDPR. Now is the time to appoint one to ensure that you get the most suitably qualified.

Currently, controllers are required to notify their data processing activities with local DPAs. Under GDPR organizations are relieved of this burden as it will not be necessary to submit notifications / registrations to each local DPA of data processing activities, nor will it be a requirement to notify / obtain approval for transfers based on the Model Contract Clauses (MCCs). Instead, there will be internal record keeping requirements and the DPO appointment will be mandatory only for those controllers and processors whose core activities consist of processing operations which require regular and systematic monitoring of data subjects on a large scale or of special categories of data or data relating to criminal convictions and offences. Importantly, the DPO according to the Article 29 Working Party they:

- Must be appointed on the basis of professional qualities and, in particular, expert knowledge on data protection law and practices
- May be a staff member or an external service provider
- Must provide their contact details to the relevant DPA
- Must be provided with appropriate resources to carry out their tasks and maintain their expert knowledge
- Must report directly to the highest level of management
- Must not carry out any other tasks that could results in a conflict of interest.

Restrictions

None of the individual rights under the GDPR are intended to be an absolute right. The definition in EU law of an absolute right refers to: "where there is an unqualified right" or "a legally enforceable right to take some action or to refrain from acting at the sole discretion of the person having the right of action".
In addition to the specific limitations set out in the GDPR, EU and member state law can provide for additional restrictions in certain circumstances, such as safeguarding of national and public security

and defence or of criminal investigations and the enforcement of civil law claims, where those restrictions are necessary and proportionate measures in a democratic society. Therefore although one of the aims for GDPR was a single harmonized regulation across all Member States there will in practice be differences that have come about due to the necessity for the regulation to be compatible with and co-exist with Member State Law.

Penalties

It would be that under the GDPR any organizations in breach of GDPR can be fined up to 4% of annual global turnover or €20 Million (whichever is greater). This is the maximum fine that can be imposed for the most serious infringements e.g. by not having sufficient customer consent to process data or violating the core of Privacy by Design concepts. There is a tiered approach to fines e.g. a company can be fined 2% for not having their records in order (article 28), not notifying the supervising authority and data subject about a breach or not conducting impact assessment. It is important to note that these rules apply to both controllers and processors -- meaning 'clouds' will not be exempt from GDPR enforcement.

Part II - Assessing GDPR Readiness & Compliance

Chapter III – GDPR Threats & Opportunities

Threats

Up until now, the introduction of GDPR has made many organisations apprehensive as they view it as more as a threat than an opportunity mainly due to the perception that:

- Many businesses that have weak data governance or data management processes are introduced to GDPR in its full complexity so they view compliance as an onerous task. For example, many IT service companies are not always clear where customer data actually resides. In addition, many organizations don't believe they can locate individual customer data quickly enough to be in compliance (30-days). To compound the problem in a survey by Forbes the findings were that less than 0.5% of the data that businesses routinely collect ever gets processed. Consequently, to ease the path to compliance these companies will need to analyse carefully what data they are collecting and how they are using it and learn the concept of minimization, purpose and transparency
- Some SMB organizations perceive challenges in ensuring data quality to achieve compliance – again this is down to insufficient data management and data flow analysis
- Apprehension of the threat that that under GDPR, an organization could face fines of up to €20m or 4% of annual worldwide turnover, whichever is greatest for data breaches.
- Perceived extra costs e.g. from implementing new systems and procedures, and from potentially having to hire the services of a DPO.
- A lack of comprehension of the scale of the cost, resources and effort needed to comply, or how far to go with compliance to satisfy regulators – a Data Flow Analysis, a

Gap analysis, followed by a Privacy Impact Assessment may go some way to resolving this situation.

Opportunities

There are several inherent advantages to bringing the organization into compliance with GDPR which may not be immediately intuitive. For example, when we look at the reasons why most organizations are apprehensive with regards GDPR it is clear that it is due to a lack of confidence in their own data governance and information management strategy and mechanisms. Often the case is cited that personal data is hard to locate in a modern IT environment but that shouldn't be the case with subjects' personal data. Similarly, not having an awareness of the location or the extent of the personal data held by an organization is a weak excuse as it would indicate a lack of management and control, which begs the question as to whether the organization should be holding the data in the first place.

By using GDPR compliance as the driver to bring the organizations data governance up to compliance levels will provide additional data security, privacy and peace of mind. Furthermore, ensuring the transparent and fair, open treatment of subjects' personal data will likely enhance the reputation of the organization and mitigate many of the threats not just from non-compliance to GDPR but also to the vast array of cyber threats an organization is faced with today.

Security commentators have pointed out that larger companies and those which store and use large amounts of data e.g. companies in the finance, health and retail sectors, are most likely to have started early almost certainly out of perceived business or compliance necessity in planning for GDPR and that is very true as they would have already been DPD compliant so the step up is not so onerous. Hence for organizations that already have their data governance, security policies and data management mechanisms in order then GDPR is not such a burden. In reality, for these organizations it can be viewed as an opportunity to revisit and confirm all the processes and procedures related to data governance and privacy compliance. Consequently, the companies that have been more proactive and have an early lead in their preparations, and / or have previously focused on privacy procedures will have a defined strategy for managing the technical and organisational measures that provide privacy. Additionally these early starter organisations will likely have enforcement/compliance procedures and policies as well as a framework in place that defines the roles and responsibilities within the organisation. These organizations therefore will be naturally at an advantage when GDPR comes into force in May 2018.

For the others especially the SMBs then some security experts suggest that the preparation for, and the focusing on compliance with GDPR could, in fact, be also an opportunity to build their own technical and organisation measures that will provide a compliance framework for the organisation. Often such a proposition will be met with a wry smile as it is fundamentally true in theory but in practice there just aren't the budgets, resources and effort available for what would be deemed a support project. However, GDPR has big teeth and can inflict bigger potential penalties and those have a way of focusing the minds of Boards. Such penalties will prove a strong motivator to executives to free up the funds to ensure there are sufficient technology and organisational measures, audits, resources and mechanisms in place to ensure the organizations compliance with GDPR. Consequently the organisation can use the resources and effort available to enhance their overall security and data management footprint introduce new data governance strategies and alter the culture of the organisation towards a more privacy and security centric stance mindset.

In addition by culture based upon the principles of fair, open and honest data processing in a transparent, privacy-friendly way it could be seen as a competitive advantage by customers and may well enhance the brand through increased reputation and trust.

Moreover by adopting good data handling practices this could help companies to avoid damage to brand reputation through security threats from other attack vectors such as the dreaded crypto-ransom attacks, data disclosures or the loss of privacy of consumers' private data.

By investing in GDPR compliance in order to mitigate the risk and limit financial and reputational damage that may occur if found wanting there will be direct spin offs as it will increase the cyber security posture of the company. These benefits will materialise through regular compliance audits, data flow analysis, which leads to an increased knowledge of the business flows and procedures which opens up a whole world of potential for increased operational efficiency. There is also the extended scope of risk assessments that will uncover the value and status of the organizations data assets.

Lastly, but not least is that even the darkest GDPR cloud may have a silver lining in so much as the requirement for unambiguous or even explicit consent in tandem with the requirement for informed and proactive opt-in by the data subject to marketing and promotional campaigns will produce a high value list of genuinely interested prospects. For this reason GDPR may well not even be too detrimental to sales and marketing campaigns as we will discuss later.

Chapter IV – Starting out with Awareness and Accountability

In addition the aims of the GDPR is very clear on *what* needs to be done to protect the Data Subject's rights, but the really important question most organisations should be asking is *how to* comply with the regulation and how they can transform the financial burden and effort required for GDPR into an investment for the future.

One thing though is very clear – If you do not need to process private data then don't because it is far more complex than it first seems.

When we consider implementing GDPR there are really two type of organizations those that are already DPD compliant or at least pretend to be and organizations that are completely new to data privacy and have no experience in compliance with the existing DPD.

It might seem strange that there could be organizations operating today that are not DPD compliant or at least attempting to be so. However that has been one of the DPD's weaknesses in so much as many organizations simply ignored it or paid only cursory lip-service to the regulations. We only have to consider the failures of 'Talk Talk' a mobile phone operator in the UK back in 2015 to see how even a major service provider with millions of subscribers could have such poor data governance, security policies and privacy management mechanisms in place. For their sins 'Talk Talk' were fined around 400,000 Euro under the DPD by the UK regulators, when GDPR is applied in 2018 that fine would be more like 50 million Euros.

Consequently, we are seeing a lot more activity from organizations eager now to comply with GDPR and few will surely be as foolhardy or reckless as to try and ignore the regulations but many due to ignorance simply will be found wanting. The problem is though that even if organisations recognise that they fall under the GDPR it isn't easy to develop a culture of diligence and competency with regards data management, information security and personal data privacy overnight.

Developing a culture of security and data privacy is especially difficult in SMBs or start ups were a culture of innovation and guerrilla marketing tactics often trumps more conventional security and privacy practices. However, with both types of organization an implementation of GDPR processes can be approached from either the top down or the bottom up. The approaches are not mutually exclusive and that a successful implementation of GDPR will almost certainly be based on a combination of these complementary approaches.

The main reason to select one approach as opposed to the other is due more to the existing organizations culture and their maturity in data security/privacy governance. For example, in a top down approach, the GDPR implementation team will analyse the business and interview stakeholders in the business units to get a clear understanding of all business (data) processes that involve personal data in order to understand the flow of personal data throughout the organization. To establish data flows for each business process that requires the collection or processing of private personal data such as credit checks, address verification, data analytics, amongst many others there are a number of data attributes that need be clarified such as:

- Has consent been obtained for this particular process?
- What is the business purpose of the collection?
- Who is the Controller?
- Who is the Processor?
- Who is the responsible Data Protection Officer?
- What is the data retention period?
- What type of data is collected?
- Is this the minimum data required?
- Who in the organization will require access to this data?
- Which third parties share this information?
- Where is the personal data stored

- How is the information stored, is the data anonomised, or Pseudonymisation
- Is the personal data stored in encrypted format at rest and in transit?
- If personal data is stored in a Processor facility (cloud computing service) and is encrypted who holds the keys?
- And these are just a few of the many other questions

The best practice process of a data flow analysis, followed by a GAP analysis and an impact assessment should not be considered as a one-time effort or a check-list activity indeed if audited and a check-list are produced as evidence of due diligence and compliance it may be looked upon with considerable suspicion. This is simply because each organisations business processes and procedures will be different indeed most organization's documented procedures and processes bear scant relation to those in practice let alone follow a common best practice for the relevant industry.

Furthermore, it is an ongoing process hence the importance of developing or nurturing a culture as once all the processes that are related to GDPR and the processing of personal data are identified and categorized, they will need to be maintained as the organization, its infrastructure and processes evolve over time.

The alternative bottom up approach is more technical in nature and more suited to technology and security aware organizations. These will be organizations that have already established data management and security processes and have mechanisms in place to mitigate data leakage of valuable data out with the business. These organizations use metadata management tools or Personal Data Management tools to identify personally identifiable information (PII) and categorize these data elements by assigning relevant attributes for GDPR. For example, any personal identifiable information in a file or email will be identified at a gateway and prevented from leaving the security boundaries of the organization. This approach requires expensive equipment and skilled implementation and it can take a long time to deploy as data must be identified and classified for GDPR however if the organization is already DPD compliant most of the heavy lifting will already have been completed.

Identifying and categorizing the data processes and elements involving personal data is however only the preparation stage. To build a process for compliance of the regulation requires companies to implement a risk based approach to the process and this involves at least a GAP analysis followed by a full PIA or Privacy Impact Assessment. For larger organization that will handle large quantities or personal data especially if it is data that are in special categories a DPIA (Data Protection Impact Assessment) will be required by GDPR. Both the PIA and the DPIA are risk assessments with some special features and they will be discussed in detail in a later chapter.

However determining the condition of the organisations readiness for GDPR compliance and identifying the processes, procedures and mechanisms that require attention is only the start. The identified data processes, data elements, attributes, risk metrics, mitigations, and technical and organisational measures will have to be governed. Not just that they must be documented and must be auditable at any time by the regulators under the accountability principles.

Accountability

What are the accountability principles?

The notion of accountability was formally introduced into data protection regulation in 1980 so it is not new to privacy law and policy. Since then however, the accountability principle has also gradually been included into national data protection laws.
While accountability is about allocating responsibility for privacy compliance, it also requires a proactive, systematic and ongoing approach to data protection and privacy compliance coming about through the implementation of privacy management programs.

The new accountability principle in Article 5 of the GDPR requires an organization to demonstrate that it complies with the principles of privacy and states explicitly that this is solely the responsibility of the organization.

How can an organization demonstrate compliance?

In order to demonstrate compliance and accountability an organization must:

- Implement appropriate technical and organisational measures that ensure and demonstrate that they do indeed comply. This may include internal data protection policies such as staff training, internal audits of processing activities, and reviews of internal Quality Management, HR and Security policies, procedures and documentation.
- To maintain relevant documentation on all processing activities separated for each Controller.
- Where appropriate, an organization should appoint a data protection officer.
- Implement measures that meet the principles of data protection by design and data protection by default. Measures could include:
    - Data minimisation;
    - Pseudonymisation;
    - Transparency;
    - Access Control;
    - Data identification and categorisation; and
    - Auditing and improving security mechanisms and processes on an ongoing basis.
- Use data protection impact assessments where appropriate.

- Adhere to approved codes of conduct and/or certification schemes.

Following those best practices and you will not go far wrong however where the GDPR gets a little hazy is when it attempts to differentiate between small and large businesses. Initially the aim was to differentiate dependent on the number of personal records that an organization processed – which would have made more sense. Unfortunately this was rejected in favour of a yardstick that measured a company by the number of its employees – which makes little sense when the regulations are about processing personal data. Still that is what was agreed and passed into legislation so that is what we have to work with.

As well as the obligation to provide comprehensive, clear and transparent privacy policies if the organisation has more than 250 employees, the organisation must maintain additional internal records of all data processing activities.

If the organisation has less than 250 employees they are exempt from many of the more stringent clauses but are still required to maintain records of activities related to higher risk processing, such as:

• processing personal data that could result in a risk to the rights and freedoms of individual; or
• processing of special categories of data or criminal convictions and offences.

What do I need to record?

An organization must maintain internal records of processing activities. Therefore it must record the following information.

- Name (Legal) and details of the organisation (and where applicable, of other controllers, the representative and data protection officer).
- Purposes of the processing.
- Description of the categories of individuals and categories of personal data.
- Document and maintain categories and recipients of personal data.(third parties sharing the data)

- Details of data transfers to third countries including documentation of the transfer mechanism and the appropriate safeguards in place.
- Data retention schedules.
- Description of technical and organisational security measures.

It is essential under GDPR that these records are diligently created and maintained as the organization may be required to make these records available to the relevant supervisory authority for purposes of an investigation.

So far we have studied the current Data Protection Directive and how those terms apply to business in the EU currently. However, all that will change in the spring of 2018 when the GDPR comes into force. The new regulation has expanded upon many of the stipulations set out within the DPD regards protecting personal data and as a result we need to address and become aware of these new mechanisms.

Awareness

The twelve principles of the GDPR

- *Awareness:* - It is essential that executives, decision makers and key stakeholders in your organisation are aware that the law is changing to the GDPR. Furthermore, in order to create a culture of privacy awareness training should be made available to relevant employees such as business leaders, project managers, product/service developers, as well as Sales & Marketing amongst others so that they appreciate the impact privacy compliance is likely to have. Awareness of the status quo of the organization is required and an audit is helpful in identifying areas that could cause compliance problems under the GDPR this is generally done through a Privacy Impact Assessment. GDPR requires a risk approach so the logical place to start is at your organisation's risk register. Implementing the GDPR could have significant budget and resource implications, especially for larger and more complex organisations.

- *Information you hold*: An organization should document what personal data they hold as this is only competent data governance. They need to document where it came from and who the data is shared with. Further in order to discover the provenance and purpose of the personal data they hold organizations may have to perform a data flow audit across the organisation. The GDPR requires that records are kept and maintained with reference to all the organizations processing activities per controller and contract.
However the GDPR takes into account data sharing in a networked world so the organization is also accountable for data they have shared or disseminated to other entities. For example, if an organization has inaccurate personal data and has shared this with another organisation, they are responsible to take action to inform the other organisation about the inaccuracy so it can correct its own records. Doing this will also help you to comply with the GDPR's accountability principle, which requires organisations to be able to show how they comply with the data protection principles, for example by having effective policies and procedures in place.

- *Communicating privacy information*: A key step that organizations will have to take is to review their current privacy notices and put a plan in place for making any necessary changes in time for GDPR implementation. Changes to the information that a Controller must supply a data subject, now require additional information such as the lawful basis for processing the data, the data retention periods and that individuals have a right to object. The GDPR requires the information to be provided and be available, in concise, easy to understand and clear language that is suitable for the target audience.

- *Individuals' rights*: an organization should check their procedures to ensure they cover all the relevant rights of individuals under the GDPR. The key points here are that the GDPR includes the following rights for individuals: the right to be informed; the right of access; the right to rectification; the right to erasure; the right to restrict processing; the right to data portability; the right to object; and the right not to be subject to automated decision-making including profiling. As these rights are mostly enhancements to the existing DPD, an organization that is already compliant will find the upgrade to the GDPR relatively straightforward. However for most organizations this should be looked at as an opportunity to check and verify their compliance procedures.
- *Subject access requests*: an organization must decide and have procedures and responsibilities in place as to who should update their procedures and plan how they will handle requests to take account of the new rules: In most cases you will need an automated system to handle incoming SAR and register and record the details. The organization can refuse or charge for requests that are manifestly unfounded or excessive but you will have to prove that was the case. If you refuse a request for information, the individual must be informed as to why and that they have the right to complain to the supervisory authority and to a judicial remedy. They must be informed of this decision and their rights to escalate the request/complain without undue delay and at the latest, within one month.
- *Lawful basis for processing personal data*: An organization should identify the lawful basis for processing a subject's activity under the GDPR, this is a pre-requisite as otherwise collection and processing would be unlawful. Therefore the organization must document the lawful purpose and update their privacy notice to explain it. Many organisations will not have thought about their lawful basis for processing personal data so this will come as a shock. GDPR extends some individuals' rights so documents and policies will require to be modified depending on your lawful basis for processing

the subject's personal data. For example, subjects' will have a stronger right to have their data deleted where you use consent as the lawful basis for processing. You will also have to explain your lawful basis for processing personal data in your privacy notice and when you answer a subject access request. The lawful bases in the GDPR are broadly the same as the conditions for processing in the DPA. This is an opportunity for the organization to review the types of processing activities they carry out and to identify their lawful basis for doing so. An organization should document all lawful bases in order to comply with the GDPR's 'accountability' requirements.

- *Consent*: The organization should review how they seek, record and manage consent and whether they need to make any changes. Importantly, the regulations are also retrospective so you will need to consider the consent for existing systems that hold personal data. This may be a big problem for organizations that currently do not comply with DPD and hold CRM systems containing databases of customer records. Hence they will be required to obtain or refresh and document personal data consents for existing systems if they don't already meet the GDPR standard. Consent must be freely given, specific, informed and unambiguous. There must be a positive opt-in – consent cannot be inferred from silence, pre-ticked boxes or assumed by inactivity. It must also be separate from other terms and conditions, and there must always be a similar or simple ways for people to withdraw consent. In addition, subjects consent has to be verifiable and individuals generally have more rights where you rely on consent to process their data. Organizations are not required to automatically 'repaper' or refresh all existing DPA consents in preparation for the GDPR. However, if there is a reliance on an individuals' consent to process their data, make sure it will meet the GDPR standard on being specific, granular, clear, and prominent, it should also be an opt-in mechanism, properly documented and easily withdrawn.

- **Rights of Children**: An organization should start thinking now about whether you need to put systems in place to verify individuals' ages and to obtain parental or guardian consent for any data processing activity. This can present major issues with those organizations supplying an online information society service. As GDPR will bring in special protection for children's personal data, particularly in the context of commercial internet services such as social networking. The GDPR sets the age when a child can give their own consent to this processing at 16 although member states can alter this age level. If a child is younger then you will need to get consent from a person holding 'parental responsibility'. To compound the problem when collecting children's data your privacy notice must be written in language that children will understand.
- *Data breaches*: It is essential that an organization should make sure they have the right procedures in place in order to detect, report and investigate a personal data breach. The GDPR introduces a duty on all organisations to report certain types of data breach to the regulatory body, and in some cases even to the data subjects. But there is only a requirement to notify the Regulator of a breach where it is likely to result in a risk to the loss of rights and freedoms of individuals – if, for example, there was significant risk of financial loss, loss of confidentiality or any other significant economic or social disadvantage. However, where a breach is unlikely to result in loss such as when data is lost or disclosed to an unauthorised third party but is encrypted then the requirements for notification of a breach are relaxed but they must still be documented no matter how small and seemingly insignificant i.e. a lost thumb drive containing a spreadsheet of a customer list. But if there is any high risk to the rights and freedoms of individuals, for example a disclosure of clear text data, then the organization must notify the regulator and will also have to notify those concerned directly in most cases. This is an onerous task that requires proactive process and procedures so could be viewed

as an opportunity to review and assess the types of personal data processed and document where it would be required to notify the Regulator or how to contact and by what method affected individuals if a breach has occurred. Failure to report a breach when required to do so could result in a heavy fine, on top of a fine for the breach itself.

- *Data Protection by Design:* The GDPR makes privacy by design an express legal requirement, under the term 'data protection by design and by default'. It also makes PIAs – referred to as 'Data Protection Impact Assessments' or DPIAs – mandatory in certain circumstances. It is good practice in implementing GDPR or even in assessing GDPR readiness to become familiar with carrying out Privacy Impact Assessments (PIA) as they should be integrated with the application, product, and system development project lifecycle. By including a PIA template into the project lifecycle at an early stage – such as during overall project risk assessment is a logic place - this should ensure the adoption of a 'privacy by design' approach to projects, products and services development. An interesting anomaly is that the GDPR refers to a Data Protection Impact Assessment (DPIA) and some documentation indicates that a DPIA is synonymous with a PIA. However that is incorrect as a DPIA has certain requirements not generally included in most PIA templates. It is important to note the distinction as a GDPR style DPIA is required in situations where data processing is likely to result in high risk to individuals, for example where a new technology is being deployed or where there is a significant profiling operation that will affect individuals such as those in special categories.

  If a DPIA indicates that the data processing is high risk, such as when processing large quantities of special category data and you cannot sufficiently address those risks, you will be required to consult the Regulator to seek its opinion as to whether the processing operation complies with the GDPR.

- *Data Protection Officers*: An organization – if required - should designate someone to take responsibility for data protection compliance and assess where this role will sit within your organisation's structure and governance arrangements. The organization only requires to designate a DPO if they are: a public authority (except for courts acting in their judicial capacity); an organisation that carries out the regular and systematic monitoring of individuals on a large scale; or an organisation that carries out the large scale processing of special categories of data, such as health records, or information about criminal convictions.

- *International scope:* If the organisation operates in more than one EU member state, you should determine and document which is the lead data protection supervisory authority. The lead authority is the supervisory authority in the Member State where the main establishment is located. The main establishment is determined to be the location where your central administration in the EU is located or else the location where decisions about the purposes and means of processing are taken and implemented for example the corporate HQ. This is only relevant where you carry out cross-border processing – i.e. the organization has establishments in more than one EU member state or they have a single establishment in the EU that carries out processing which substantially affects individuals in other EU states. If this applies to your organisation, you should map out where your organisation makes its most significant decisions about its processing activities. This will help to determine your 'main establishment' and therefore your lead supervisory authority.

Chapter IV – Data Governance & Privacy Management

As we have seen the GDPR mandates a "Risk Based Approach:" through Privacy Impact Assessments and where appropriate the higher standard of a Data Impact and Privacy Assessment. An organization's controls must be developed according to the degree of risk associated with the processing activities they undertake.

Where appropriate, privacy impact assessments must be performed with the focus on protecting the data subject rights. Therefore, data protection safeguards must be designed into products and services from the earliest stage of development and hence the phrase we will hear a lot of in GDPR - Privacy by Design and by Default.

Privacy-friendly techniques such as Pseudonymisation which is the generic term GDPR uses for data obfuscating techniques such as encryption or mathematical hashing are encouraged, to reap the benefits of big data innovation while protecting privacy.

There is also an increased emphasis on record keeping for controllers – all designed to help demonstrate and meet compliance with the regulation and improve the capabilities of organisations to manage privacy and data effectively.

The requirement for Consent

We revisit the principle of consent once more and probably will again before we are done as it is a key pillar in the GDPR. Although many organization within and out with the European Community have already adopted privacy processes and procedures consistent with the Data Protection Directive, the GDPR contains a number of enhanced existing protections as well as a few new ones for EU data subjects and the expansion and strengthening of the existing principle of consent is one of the more significant.

Consent remains a lawful basis to transfer personal data under the GDPR; however, the definition of consent is significantly restricted. Where Directive 95/46/EC allowed controllers to rely on implicit and "opt-out" consent in some circumstances, the GDPR requires the data subject to signal agreement by "a statement or a clear affirmative action." The new law maintains the distinct requirements for processing "special categories of personal data" that were present in the Directive, but it expands the range of what is included in those special categories.

Finally, the GDPR introduces restrictions on the ability of children to consent to data processing without parental authorization. However that clause has raised some issues in receiving consent itself and has had to be altered to allow some latitude to the Member States in setting the minimum age limit for a child to provide consent.

One of the key principles of the GDPR is that it focuses on the data protection rights of the individual and so to that end it aims to expand the requirements and restrictions for organizations in obtaining data subject consent.

The GDPR by design sets a high standard for obtaining an individual's consent, and the biggest challenge to organizations will be implementing these requirements in practice and updating their consent mechanisms. The GDPR is clearer that the DPD and expands upon what it deems an indication of consent. Consent, under the GDPR must be unambiguous and involve a clear affirmative action – inaction is not acceptable as an indication of consent neither is the requirement to opt-out acceptable. As an example, of affirmative action the GDPR specifically bans pre-ticked opt-in boxes. Furthermore, consent should be separate from other terms and conditions. It should not generally be a precondition of signing up to a service or continuing to use a service. In addition an organization requires informing the individual of each purpose and obtaining granular consent for each distinct processing operation. The organization must also keep clear records to demonstrate consent.

As the GDPR stresses the importance of fair, open, and honest methods in obtaining an individual's consent it also gives the data subject the specific right to withdraw their consent at any time. Therefore an organization will need to inform people about their right to withdraw their consent, and offer them easy mechanisms in order for them to exercise their right to withdraw consent at any time. Furthermore and very importantly and is often overlooked the consent must be given with the individual's free will.

This is where consent can become somewhat controversial as there must be an equality and balance between the organization seeking consent and the individual providing the consent for there to exist conditions compatible with free will. The GDPR believes that consent cannot meet the expected standards or definition of free will in a situation where there is an obvious imbalance of authority. Hence in GDPR there is the principle that consent will not, or cannot, be freely given if there is an imbalance in the relationship between the individual and the controller. In this respect some Public authorities, employers and other organisations in a position of power are likely to find it more difficult to get valid consent as it could be deemed to contradict the conditions required for the principle of free will.

To compound the issue consent applies to all systems, legacy systems as well as new post GDPR systems so this means in many cases affirming the lawful consent for individual personal data records on existing CRM or HR systems for example will be necessary. If however consent has been obtained and importantly has been documented and can thus be demonstrated for any legacy systems then that prior consent will suffice for the purpose of GDPR and does not need to be refreshed. Therefore the onus is firmly with the organization to review existing consents and update their consent mechanisms and documentation to ensure that they meet the GDPR standard.

What are the key changes to obtaining consent in practice?

An organization will need to review their consent mechanisms to make sure they meet the GDPR requirements on being specific, granular, be in clear language, prominently placed, require affirmative action, require an opt-in, be verifiable, documented and importantly be easily withdrawn. Therefore some of the key new points that require addressing are as follows:

- Unbundled: consent requests must be separate from other terms and conditions. Consent should not be a precondition of signing up to a service unless necessary for that service.

- Active opt-in: pre-ticked opt-in boxes are invalid – use un-ticked opt-in boxes or similar active opt-in methods so long as it is a binary choice with each option given equal prominence

- Granular: give granular options to consent separately to different types of processing wherever appropriate.

- Named: name your organisation and any third parties who will be relying on consent – even precisely defined categories of third-party organisations will not be acceptable under the GDPR they must be identified by name.

- Documented: keep records to demonstrate what the individual has consented to, including what they were told, and when and how they consented.

- Easy to withdraw: inform individuals to their right to withdraw their consent at any time, and how to do this. A key principle here is that it must be as easy to withdraw as it was to give consent. This means you will need to have simple and effective withdrawal mechanisms prominently placed and not hidden away in the small print.

Consent is only one of the bases for legal processing there are other options that should be explored such as legitimate interests, necessary execution of a contract and some other options. The common misconception is that "explicit" consent is generally required for all categories. However that isn't true as "explicit" is not one of the attributes the GDPR attaches to consent for the standard categories of personal data. Explicit consent is required for the special categories as they require the protection of a higher standard.

According to GDPR articles consent means "any freely given, specific, informed and unambiguous indication of his or her wishes by which the data subject, either by a statement or by a clear affirmative action, signifies agreement to personal data relating to them being processed;"

There is no mention of "explicit" in the GDPR definition of what they mean by consent only that it should be freely given, informed and unambiguous. However although the consent itself need not be explicit –albeit it must be signalled through a statement or by a clear affirmative action, the purposes for which the consent is gained does need to be "collected for specified, explicit and legitimate purposes".

Consequently, the requirement is to explicitly inform the data subject as to the specific purpose that their data is going to be used and this must be provided at the point of data collection.

For marketers, and those organizations that are involved in the monitoring of individuals online behaviour and activity in particular there has been much debate about the type of consent that might be required under GDPR.

After all consent need not be explicit but an individual's consent should be demonstrable – hence an organisation needs to be able to show clearly how the consent was obtained, as well as how and when the consent was applied to a specific purpose.

The problem however of using an alternative to consent which circumnavigates the thorny issue that consent must be informed, freely given, and easily withdrawn is that the alternatives also provide significant hurdles to lawful processing of personal data. For example, if an organisation relies instead of consent on contract requirement, i.e. processing of the data is necessary under the contractual obligations then that will nicely avoid having to seek consent. But there is an issue in that the organisation will be strictly limited to the data that is necessary to perform the objectives of the contract – after all the controller (a marketer, or a behaviour monitor) cannot insist on collecting personal data that's not required for the performance of a contract as a pre-requisite for that contract. However for other entities and organisations contractual obligations is a neat solution to the conundrum of the imbalance in the relationship precluding consent being freely given.

GDPR mandates affirmative consent for data processing

Under the GDPR, consent must be "freely given, specific, informed and unambiguous." There was uncertainty leading up to the final draft of the GDPR whether the EU would settle on "unambiguous" consent as existed under the current Data Protection Directive, or the higher standard of "explicit" consent. The GDPR eventually after much discussion opted for retaining the standard of unambiguous consent, while requiring such consent to be expressed "by a statement or by a clear affirmative action."

The regulation clarifies that an affirmative action signalling consent may include ticking a box on a website, "choosing technical settings for information society services," or "another statement or conduct" that clearly indicates assent to the processing. "Silence, pre-ticked boxes or inactivity," however, is presumed inadequate to confer consent.

The GDPR removes the possibility of an opt-out option by requiring the data subject to make a statement or provide a clear affirmative action. In particular, the GDPR includes three additional requirements:

1. GDPR gives data subjects the right to withdraw consent at any time and "it shall be as easy to withdraw consent as to give it." Controllers must inform data subjects of the right to withdraw before consent is given. Once consent is withdrawn, data subjects have the right to have their personal data erased and no longer used for processing.
2. GDPR adds a presumption that consent is *not* freely given if there is "a clear imbalance between the data subject and the controller, in particular where the controller is a public authority." Importantly, a controller may not make a service

       conditional upon consent, unless the processing is necessary for the service.
3. The GDPR adds that consent must be specific to each data processing operation. To meet the specificity requirement under Article 7, a request for consent to data processing must be "clearly distinguishable" from any other matters in a written document, and it must be provided "in an intelligible and easily accessible form, using clear and plain language."

However, there are as always some exceptions and GDPR exempts controllers from obtaining consent for subsequent processing operations if the operations are deemed to be "compatible."

Now, how GDPR defines the use of compatible is best described with reference to Recital 50, which states that compatibility is determined by looking at factors including the link between the processing purposes, the reasonable expectations of the data subject, the nature and consequences of further processing, and the existence of appropriate safeguards for the data.

There are also exceptions to consent and indeed allows additional processing for archiving in the public interest, which is defined by the Member State, as well as for statistical purposes or scientific and historical research, which will generally be considered compatible, and, therefore, exempt from specific consent.

What this means is that the exemption allowed for compatible purpose is potentially quite broad and open to abuse. For example potentially controllers will not have to erase or rectify data after the data subject has withdrawn their consent as it may be compatible with another purpose. It also has the potential to impact upon the restrictions on processing, data portability and the data subject's rights to object to and to be notified of processing operations.

There are other potential loop-holes in the GDPR regulations one of which relates to the current e-Privacy Directive relating to cookies and other tracking technologies. The Directive states that a data subject must provide specific, informed consent to the use of cookies or comparable tracking technology. However, the GDPR provides an exception where cookies are "strictly necessary for the legitimate purpose of enabling the use of a specific service requested by the subscriber or user." It also provides that "the user's consent to processing may be expressed by using the appropriate settings of a browser or other application."

The Article 29 Working Party's interpretation of this provision is that the browser settings exception will apply only in the case where the browser's default configuration rejects the placement of cookies. In this specific case the user can actively opt-in to receiving cookies by adjusting the default configuration of the browser. Hence, this action would be in accord with the GDPR's requirement of "a clear affirmative action."

Despite there being several potential loop-holes in the GDPR the onus always falls on a controller that relies on consent as a basis for processing to demonstrate that consent was obtained lawfully according to the principles of the GDPR.

GDPR requires explicit consent for special categories of personal data

GDPR requires a higher level of consent – "explicit" consent – for the processing of "special categories of personal data." These special categories relate to personal data that are "particularly sensitive in relation to fundamental rights and freedoms" and, therefore, "deserve specific protection." They include data "revealing racial or ethnic origin, political opinions, religious or philosophical beliefs, or trade-union membership, and the processing of genetic data, biometric data for the purpose uniquely identifying a natural person, data concerning health or data concerning a natural person's sex life or sexual orientation."

The standard under Directive 95/46/EC, which is currently the law also required controllers to obtain explicit consent for processing special categories of personal data. The Directive defined explicit consent as "all situations where individuals are presented with a proposal to agree or disagree to a particular use or disclosure of their personal information and they respond actively to the question, orally or in writing."

In the case of explicit consent, a user's conduct or choice of browser settings probably will not be sufficient to meet this high level of consent. In addition the GDPR also allows member states to enact laws that restrict the processing of some categories of data *even if* the data subject explicitly consents.

The only distinction between the Directive and the GDPR on this issue is that the GDPR expands the definition of sensitive data to include genetic data, biometric data, and data concerning sexual orientation. Genetic data is defined, under Article 4, as "personal data relating to the inherited or acquired genetic characteristics of natural persons which give unique information about the physiology or the health of that natural person and which result, in particular, from an analysis of a biological sample from the natural person in question." Biometric data is personal data that identifies an individual based on the "specific technical processing" of the individual's physical or behavioural characteristics. However, an interesting aside is the question of when is a photograph considered to be a bio-metric image? Recital 51 notes that photographs will qualify as biometric data only when they are processed "through a specific technical means allowing the unique identification or authentication of a natural person." This could have future unintended ramifications for Big Data and Machine Learning training algorithms.

GDPR requires parental consent for processing children's personal data

GDPR introduces specific protections for children by limiting their ability to consent to data processing without parental authorization. The final draft opted for the age of consent to be set at 16 years, but it allows Member States to set a lower age but not below 13 years. Thus, unless otherwise provided by a Member State's law, controllers must obtain the consent of a parent or guardian when processing the personal data of a child under the age of 16. There is an additional requirement that they must make "reasonable efforts" to verify that a parent or guardian has provided the appropriate consent.

Several member states during the drafting of the regulation have taken umbrage with the age of consent being set at 16. The rationale behind the complaint was due to the differing rules being put in place between the EU standard and the COPPA age 13 rule applicable in the U.S. Some Member States argued that this could create significant challenges for organizations that offer international internet services. As a result several Member States the UK being one opted out of this clause and set their own age of consent to 13 in order to be compatible with US organisations.

Other Provisions *where explicit consent is required*

The GDPR requires the data subject's *explicit* consent in two other circumstances. Controllers need to obtain explicit consent to make decisions about the data subject "based solely on automated processing, including profiling." Controllers also must seek explicit consent, to authorize transfers of personal data to countries that do not provide an adequate level of protection, if no other transfer mechanism is in place.

Information Provided at Data Collection

The information that must be made available to a Data Subject by a Controller when data is collected has been strongly defined and includes;

- the identity and the contact details of the controller and DPO
- the purposes of the processing for which the personal data are intended
- the legal basis of the processing.
- where applicable the legitimate interests pursued by the controller or by a third party;

- where applicable, the recipients or categories of recipients of the personal data;
- where applicable, that the controller intends to transfer personal data internationally
- the period for which the personal data will be stored, or if this is not possible, the criteria used to determine this period;
- the existence of the right to access, rectify or erase the personal data;
- the right to data portability;
- the right to withdraw consent at any time;
- and the right to lodge a complaint to a supervisory authority;

Importantly where the data has not been obtained directly from the data subject – perhaps using a 3rd party list – the list varies and includes many headaches for marketers and those building products that aggregate marketing lists and databases of profiled individuals' personal data.

Breach & Notification

According to the regulation a "personal data breach" is "a breach of security leading to the accidental or unlawful destruction, loss, alteration, unauthorised disclosure of, or access to, personal data transmitted, stored or otherwise processed"

Data breaches do not necessarily mean that an organizations system security has be compromised by a malicious third party. It is just as much a breach if a laptop or thumb-drive is lost that contains spreadsheets or similar data sources of individual personal data such as a customer detail list or a payroll. It's also important to note that the wilful destruction or alteration of data by an employee is also a breach.

In the event of a personal data breach data controllers must notify the appropriate supervisory authority "without undue delay and, where feasible, not later than 72 hours after having become aware of it." If notification is not made within 72 hours, the controller must provide a "reasoned justification" for the delay.

The GDPR provides exceptions to this additional requirement to notify data subjects in the following circumstances:

The controller has "implemented appropriate technical and organisational protection measures" that "render the data unintelligible to any person who is not authorised to access it, such as encryption"

Notice is not required if "the personal data breach is unlikely to result in a risk for the rights and freedoms of individuals," For example if the information is encrypted so for example an attacker may have access to the database list of passwords but if these are all hashed – as they should be – then the password has not been disclosed. Therefore there is a very strong case for ensuring that all personal data is kept encrypted as this will mitigate many of the obligations to notify the regulators within the onerous 72 hour period.

Should the controller determine that the personal data breach "is likely to result in a high risk to the rights and freedoms of individuals," it must also communicate information regarding the personal data breach to the affected data subjects and this must be done "without undue delay."

In addition to the case where the controller encrypts the personal data that they hold they can also be exempt from the notification timescale of 72 hours if they can:

- "ensure that the high risk for the rights and freedoms of data subjects" is unlikely to materialise.
- When notification to each data subject would "involve disproportionate effort," in which case alternative communication measures may be used.

Importantly there is a differentiation between the breach notification obligations of the processor in contrast to the controller. For when a data processor experiences a personal data breach, it must notify the controller but otherwise has no other notification or reporting obligation.

Chapter V – Monitoring and Profiling

The GDPR introduces some new obligations on such matters as data subject consent, data anonymisation, breach notification, trans-border data transfers, and appointment of data protection officers, amongst many others which will require organizations handling EU citizens' data to undertake major operational reform.

One of the principles of keen interest is that the GDPR restricts "profiling" and gives data subjects significant rights to avoid profiling-based decisions. This seems to be a regulation article which has perhaps more profound implications than appears at first glance.

To understand the dilemma the current Data Protection Directive was implemented nearly 20 years ago, and since then technologies have proliferated that allow data controllers to gather personal data and analyze it for a variety of purposes. Several of these purposes have included the monetisation of data by actively harvesting personal data in bulk and using algorithms to gain insight to data subjects in order to potentially target them for sales and marketing.

Although the concepts of "profiling" or "target marketing" appear in the Directive, the precise terms do not. Therefore, the GDPR goes much further in its desire to contain many of these practices and places restrictions on automated data processing especially on the automated decision-based systems that can be characterized as being based upon profiling.

Data Subject Profiling

The GDPR defines profiling as any automated processing of personal data, which can be used to determine certain criteria about a person. "In particular to analyse or predict aspects concerning that natural person's performance at work, economic situation, health, personal preferences, interests, reliability, behaviour, location or movements".

This is certain to impact on some marketing processes and services although there is currently a lot of debate as to the full extent of this impact may have. There is also some related debate as to the semantics as to where the borders are drawn between profiling and selection? For example with full personalisation and other advert serving techniques these rely on a degree of selection, which is normally built on profiles of behaviour or purchase, an example being Amazon's prediction of products that the user might like, so will GDPR require consent for this now?

Furthermore, individuals have the right not to be subject to the results of automated decision making, including profiling, which produces legal effects on him/her or otherwise significantly affects them. Thus, individuals can opt out of profiling if they wish.

Importantly, GDPR stipulates that the use of automated decision making systems will be legal only where individuals have explicitly consented to its use, or if profiling is necessary under a contract between an organisation and an individual, or if profiling is authorised by the EU or a Member State Law. This raises a lot of questions as to how the GDPR will face up to the challenge of machine learning and Artificial Intelligence algorithms which are becoming pervasive within society as these work almost entirely as automated profiling systems and worse than their ubiquity is that their value is in their autonomous decision making.

Defining profiling

The GDPR raises the bar for individual privacy by defining regulations aimed at the "profiling" of individuals. The restrictions though are not as severe as originally proposed and have ultimately been adopted in a much narrower scope.

Under GDPR, data processing may be characterized as "profiling" when it involves (a) automated processing of personal data; and (b) using that personal data to evaluate certain personal aspects relating to a natural person. Specific examples include analyzing or predicting "aspects concerning that natural person's performance at work, economic situation, health, personal preferences, interests, reliability, behaviour, location or movements."

This definition implicitly excludes data processing that is not "automated."

The GDPR elaborates on the definition of Profiling by adding that any processing activity involves data subject "monitoring" when "individuals are tracked on the Internet including potential subsequent use of data processing techniques which consist of profiling an individual, particularly in order to take decisions concerning her or him or for analysing or predicting her or his personal preferences, behaviours and attitudes."

This definition by the GDPR would suggest that profiling is not just monitoring or tracking, but instead is something more substantial, involving the intention to *take decisions* regarding a data subject or *predict* the subject's behaviours and preferences.

That "profiling" requires some sort of purpose rather than just monitoring or tracking an individual is demonstrated by the data subject's rights to be informed of the "consequences" of profiling decisions. The GDPR articles address what information must be provided to a data subject upon personal data collection. Also, there is a requirement to provide certain information upon the data subject's request for clarification of their data's purpose. In either scenario there is a requirement to disclose "the existence of automated decision making including profiling" along with "the significance and the envisaged consequences of such processing for the data subject."

Furthermore the GDPR gives clues to its target audience when it establishes its jurisdiction over non-EU controllers provided they are "monitoring the behaviour of [EU] data subjects as far as their behaviour takes places within the European Union."

As the aims of the GDPR are focused upon individual privacy rights, it provides data subjects the right to object to processing for direct marketing as well as to "profiling to the extent it is related to direct marketing,"

For organizations that are collecting data related to profiling or automated decision making the GDPR describes the obligation to conduct a data impact assessment and characterizes the "profiling of data" as follows: "A data protection impact assessment should also be made where personal data are *processed for taking decisions* regarding specific natural persons *following any systematic and extensive evaluation of personal aspects relating to natural persons* based on profiling those data."

By considering the articles in relation to "profiling" together, they seem to consistently require not simply the gathering of personal data involving personal aspects of natural persons, but also the essential element of automated processing of such data for the purpose of making decisions about the data subjects.

Controllers must honour data subjects' rights regarding profiling

When we consider that profiling, taking all of the definitions and discussions into consideration is different to the collection of individual's personal data and has a consequence for that individual as an end product the GDPR gives data subjects a number of rights with regard to profiling. The rights that data subjects receive, some of which require procedures similar to those for non-profiling data processing, for example, notice and access. Others are extended such as the right to object, and to halt the profiling, or even to avoid profiling-based decisions altogether and these rights will require special processes for compliance.

Restrictions on profiling-based decisions producing legal effects

As GDPR provides data subjects with some rights, notably not necessarily to avoid profiling itself, but rather to avoid being "subject to a decision based solely on automated processing, including profiling, which produces legal effects concerning him or her or similarly significantly affects him or her." The GDPR provides as examples the "automatic refusal of an on-line credit application or e-recruiting practices without any human intervention." The example here shows that the online profiling and automated system is not the issue it is the decision making mechanism without any human intervention that is the real issue.

The GDPR text clarifies that the *decision* may nonetheless be made provided it is (a) necessary for entering into, or performance of, a contract between the data subject and a data controller; (b) authorized by Union or member state law to which the controller is subject and which also lays down suitable measures to safeguard the data subject's rights and freedoms and legitimate interests; or (c) based on the data subject's explicit consent.

However despite those exceptions there remain even in the case of a decision made pursuant to a contract with the data subject or his explicit consent, the controller must still allow the data subject to contest the decision.

There are cases where profiling decision-based processing is not allowed and the GDPR rules that profiling-based decisions shall not be based on special categories of personal data (e.g. racial, ethnic, or religious information) unless (a) the data subject has given explicit consent to the processing of those personal data for one or more specified purposes, except where prohibited by Union law or Member State law; or (b) processing is necessary for reasons of substantial public interest, on the basis of Union or Member State law. Even in these circumstances, the controller must still ensure "suitable measures to safeguard the data subject's rights and freedoms and legitimate interests are in place."

For all permissible profiling, the GDPR compels a controller to use appropriate mathematical or statistical procedures, implement technical and organisational measures to correct personal data inaccuracies and avoid errors, secure all personal data, and minimize the risk of "discriminatory effects against natural persons on the basis of racial or ethnic origin, political opinion, religion or beliefs, trade union membership, genetic or health status, or sexual orientation."

Notice and access

Under the GDPR articles the controller must inform a data subject at the time data is collected not only of the fact that profiling will occur, but as well "the logic involved" and "the envisaged consequences of such processing." Further a data subject may also inquire of a controller and receive confirmation of any such processing, including profiling and its consequences, at any time.

Profiling must cease upon objection

If a data subject exercises their right to object, and they can do this at any time the controller even when profiling is otherwise lawful must cease unless the controller demonstrates "compelling legitimate grounds for the processing which override the interests, rights and freedoms of the data subject."

When processing is for direct marketing purposes, including profiling, the data subject similarly has a right to object but in this case processing must cease and the controller is not authorized to continue under any circumstances.

Data impact assessments for controllers engaged in profiling

One of the triggers requiring a data impact assessment is when a controller engages in "a systematic and extensive evaluation of personal aspects relating to natural persons which is based on automated processing, including profiling, and on which decisions are based that produce legal effects concerning the individual or similarly significantly affect the individual."

The wording in this article underlines that although "profiling" involves more than merely automated processing, that may or may not produce legal effects or significantly affect an individual, but, when it does the data subject is entitled to additional rights and protection.

Legitimate Interests & Direct Marketing

The regulation specifically recognises that the processing of data for "direct marketing purposes" can be considered as a legitimate interest.

Legitimate interest is one of the grounds, like consent, that an organisation can use in order to process data and satisfy the principle that data has been fairly and lawfully processed.

The act says that processing is lawful if "processing is necessary for the purposes of the legitimate interests pursued by the controller or by a third party, except where such interests are overridden by the interests or fundamental rights and freedoms of the data subject which require protection of personal data, in particular where the data subject is a child."

It's worthy of note that "Direct Marketing" has not been defined – so consideration should be given to the precise nature of the marketing activity proposed to be covered by this grounds for processing.

It may, for example, mean that a simple mailing of similar goods and services to existing customers and prospects is completely legitimate without direct consent – but it certainly doesn't include "Profiling" for marketing purposes which does require consent.

Chapter VI – Performing a Privacy Impact Assessment

For many organizations GDPR preparation will take time and will not be as straightforward as taking an IT checklist approach. Unfortunately, as there already has been a two year period for preparation and transition between GDPR coming into force on May 25th 2016 and GDPR being applied in law on 26th May 2018 you have to be ready. The problem is that knowing whether your organization is GDPR ready or not is no easy task. Therefore you will need to perform a GDPR Readiness Assessment to help uncover any privacy and security gaps in order to recommend a remediation plan. Ideally, for organisation new to the Regulations a GDPR Readiness Assessment should provide the means to accelerate compliance with several of the key GDPR data-protection obligations.

Privacy and protection of the individual is the impetus for the GDPR in this the contemporary era of the internet where cloud, mobile computing, big-data platforms and the Internet of Things (IoT) have all heightened the challenge of securing citizens rights to privacy. And within this context, organizations have never been more aware of the need to protect sensitive personal data albeit with little incentive to do so. However the GDPR is designed to provide that incentive for organisations to respect and conduct their operations with the rights of the individual to mind. To this end the GDPR has strengthened the rights of the individual and extended the protection of the special categories of personal data, which could include national IDs, email addresses, or location data as well as biometric, physical, physiological, genetic or health data amongst an ever growing list of categories designated as sensitive personal data.

The EU GDPR attempts to protect individuals and their personal data through unified, modernized standards, and a set of meaningful rights for individuals. Some of the important GDPR obligations include as we have already covered the requirements of consent, which mandates that organizations obtain explicit consent to gather special category information from individuals (known as data subjects)—and be able to prove that they have done so. Additionally, consent is limited to specific purposes, and data subjects have the right to withdraw consent at any time.

GDPR also expands the current Right to Access and obtain data, allowing data subjects to request access to information held about them, and to learn how it is accessed, the purpose of the access, where it is being accessed, what categories of data are being accessed and who has access.

Complementary to the Right of Access is the Right to Erasure, often commonly referred to as the Right to be Forgotten, which provides data subjects the right to request the deletion of personal data, under certain conditions, if they do not wish to allow its use. There is also Rights to Object, which are designated to data subjects which enables them to object to data profiling and interestingly being subjected to automated decision making processes – which are becoming pervasive in contemporary business. These data subject rights raise a daunting question: How does an organization get started on a GDPR compliance program and successfully meet its obligations?

Assessing GDPR Readiness

The first steps to take on the quest for GDPR compliance are in recognising if the organization actually falls under the auspice of the GDPR as not all organizations will do. Therefore, the first aim is to establish the organization's status with regards their obligations under the new regulations.

This may seem obvious but many organisations start out on the road to compliance when they really didn't need too. If only they had examined the customer data which they held and asked themselves do we really need this data and for what purpose, they could have saved themselves a lot of time, money and effort.

Therefore, the initial process for readiness should examine the purpose and necessity for processing data and by processing we mean just about anything including collecting, handling, sharing, storing, managing, governing or securing the information. It might be surprising to discover that much of the data being processed is old, stale and worthless as it was collected as part of a long dead initiative. However even data being collected for active or long term projects such as CRM or a Big Data initiative may be irrelevant to the organization and is being collected without any obvious current purpose or need. This issue originally arose due to poorly designed default settings on applications such as CRM that provided fields for far too much personal information to be collected. However in recent years the emergence of the Big Data revolution and the cult of 'Data is the new oil' have exacerbated the problem of organisations harvesting and hoarding vast quantities of data that will never likely get processed – by them anyway – and is not even part of their business model.

Therefore, if the organisation does not need to process personal data then don't, if they must, then limit it to what is strictly necessary, secure the data robustly using encryption or hashing and restrict access to only those that have an essential business requirement and lawful purpose.

However, as easy as that is to say it is a lot more complicated in practice and hence the requirement to perform a GDPR Readiness Assessment. The goal of a Readiness Assessment is twofold: (1) identify areas of risk, and (2) design processes for mitigating those risks. The assessment results can then form the foundation for a GDPR roadmap that should support four key activities to help manage and protect personal data. (1). Assess data protection readiness to identify and mitigate security vulnerabilities. (2) Discover and classify personal data. (3) Implement controller and processor governance to track where personal data is processed and create an audit trail. (4) Manage personal data breaches and notify the organization if and when a breach occurs.

The need for a GDPR Readiness Assessment should not be viewed as an onerous task but rather as a catalyst for organizational change in culture. It can be promoted as an opportunity to reassess and think smarter about data governance and protection and the positive impacts of a solid approach to data security, privacy and protection.

The Readiness Assessment can help provide the answers to some of the key questions about personal data access and control that the GDPR mandates. It can help identify and mitigate security vulnerabilities, identify threats and security holes, as well as aid in the discovery to where personal data is located – as many organizations have no idea.

A Readiness Assessment can also provide a means of visualizing the organisation's data strategy, where data is categorised and stored, how personal data is being protected and under what Pseudonymisation policy, such as encryption, redaction or blocking. Visualisation of the organisations data governance and management mechanisms is only feasible after fully investigating and collecting operational status information. Remember consulting documented procedures are not enough, you have to check that the processes and procedures claimed to be in place are actually being followed as often as not the similarities between the documented procedures and the as-performed procedures are merely coincidental.

The second major step after performing the high level Readiness Assessment is to perform a Data Flow Analysis as this provides insight into how personal data flows through an organisation and is a pre-requisite for a Privacy Impact Assessment. A Data Flow Analysis will require an in depth examination of organisation workflows and reveal the why, when, where, who, and how, of personal data flows within the organization. A Data Flow Analysis by itself can be extremely revealing as to potential shortfalls and high risk processes.

A Data Flow Analysis is essential as it highlights the flow and the actions performed and by the entities performing the actions and this enables gaps or anomalies in the privacy process to be discovered. Again the Data Flow Analysis must be conducted by observing real world transactions and actual workflow processes and not by relying on the authenticity of any Quality ISO9001/Procedures/Workflow documentation.

Privacy Impact Assessment

GDPR insists that a risk approach should be implemented by organizations seeking compliance with the regulations. Therefore it can be considered a good practice when assessing GDPR readiness to consider the inherent risk that is present and a Privacy Impact Assessment or PIA is the tool that is used for that purpose. The PIA is a risk assessment with some minor differences; therefore if you are accomplished in performing security risk assessments then a PIA will hold no fears for your organization.

However there are a couple of caveats, (1) is that the focus is on the Data Subject and their rights of privacy not on the organisation so the evaluation of Likelihood of occurrence and Impact is from the Data Subject's perspective. (2) You must understand the difference between a Privacy Impact Assessment and the GDPR's own home grown version called the Data Protection Impact Assessment (DPIA).

PIA vs. DIPA

The terms PIA and DPIA are often mistakenly taken to be synonymous but they are actually two separate but closely related risk-based assessment tools.

The PIA (Privacy Impact Assessment) as its name suggests is primarily concerned with the risk assessment and subsequent evaluation of any negative impact to an individual's privacy. PIAs have been in use in business, commerce and industry for decades and there are several well known and proven methodologies and templates available on the Internet. Importantly, a Privacy Impact Assessment is a broad risk assessment tool that is designed to encompass all dimensions of an individual's privacy – not just their data.

Consequently a PIA focus is on the impact of all the dimensions of an individual's privacy such as:

- privacy of the physical person
- privacy of personal communications
- privacy of personal behaviour
- privacy of personal experience
- privacy of personal identifiable data (PII)

Generally a Privacy Impact Assessment also has some other characteristics and attributes that distinguish it from the vast array of other risk-based assessments such as a PIA has a broader scope in relation to the dimensions of privacy (Clarke 1997), enabling consideration of privacy of the person, privacy of personal behaviour and privacy of personal communications, as well as privacy of personal data. In addition a PIA has broad scope in relation to the expectations against which privacy impacts are compared, including people's aspirations and social norms and values in addition to any legal requirements. Therefore a PIA can be considered to be distinct from a compliance assessment.

On the other hand a DPIA (Data Protection Impact Assessment) is an altogether different beast as it can be categorised as a compliance assessment tool. After all the DPIA is the product of the GDPR Article 35 which has a tight focus on GDPR compliance of processes and practices that implement the GDPR. Therefore the DPIA is only concerned with one of the dimensions of personal privacy that of the individuals personal data.

Consequently, it is a good strategy to perform a PIA during the assessment of an organization during the GDPR readiness phase as few if any of the GDPR requirements for compliance will be in place. However, the PIA will uncover any shortcomings and gaps in the processes and procedures related to an individual's overall privacy. This forms the basis for building a solid foundation based upon individual privacy before you need to drill down and focus tightly on individual GDPR principles and clauses within the regulation.

The problem that may arise and it can become a serious issue if there is ambiguity between whether the organisation performs an PIA or a DPIA is that they may diligently perform a PIA and mitigate risk with respect to an individual's privacy across the entire privacy domain yet still fall afoul of GDPR compliance.

This is due to the GDPR's compliance assessment tool the DPIA having some very specific requirements that are not generally included or not generally stressed in most PIA templates such as the need for extensive documentation and the requirement to be able to verify the results, conclusions and mitigations applied and/or the reasons why any identified threats were not mitigated, the reasoning behind the decision and the names of those that made the decision - should the Regulator so require.

Performing a PIA for GDPR Readiness

The first stages that require to be undertaken in completing a PIA are to gain a complete understanding of how personal data is presently handled within the organization. This is where the Data Flow Analysis – which is really a required pre-requisite of any PIA – is invaluable. If for whatever reason there is no Data Flow Analysis then you will need to perform that function as part of the PIA, which is becoming a standard way for organizations to assess GDPR readiness.

There are many diverse approaches to performing a PIA and much depends on the culture and maturity of the organization with respect to security, privacy and importantly their data governance. The different approaches in the way PIAs are conducted demonstrate that there is no one right way of performing impact assessments so they need to be adapted to the project and the organisation on a case by case basis.

However, there are some common steps across the array of diverse approaches that are useful in guiding organisations on what they should be doing. How an organisation whether that be a Controller, Processor or both, decide to implement the steps in the PIA structure

will vary depending on the business and the existing project and risk management framework(s) that are already in place.
However, a general framework for a Privacy Impact Assessment that could be incorporated within a project life-cycle is as follows.

1. Understand and document the personal data flows

The first step in the PIA process — and an on-going one when completing a PIA — is to understand and document what personal data are being processed, why they are being processed (the purpose) and to understand the data flows. Some useful questions to ask as a starting point are:

- what personal data will be collected/ captured;
- why will this personal data be collected/captured;
- who will they be processed by (who will have access);
- who will they be shared with;
- where will they be processed and stored; and
- when will they no longer be needed?

It is best if these questions are included in a form for project owners to complete at the beginning of the project, or as prompts for discussion in initial project meetings/privacy consultations.

Performing the discovery phase of this type of information fits in well with initial Project Management Life-Cycles where the initial stage is discovering and collecting information. Hence, collecting and collating the answers to these questions can be less challenging and time-consuming as it involves working with many parts of the organisation.

2. Check legal compliance

Once there is an initial understanding of the projects data requirements, the purpose of the processing, and the personal data flows of the project the next step is to consider the legal status with respect to compliance. This step is once more most effective when carried out early on in the project's life-cycle as it is an opportunity to manage and perhaps it may temper the expectation of stakeholders with regards personal data collection and to what legally can or cannot be collected for the purposes of processing. By managing customer/stakeholder expectations early and gaining consensus it can prevent conflict later and thereby allows the project to be structured in a legally compliant manner.

The significant aim of this stage of the PIA entails an assessment of the necessity and proportionality of the processing but without neglecting the other core principles. For example, how the notice requirements are achieved, which condition(s) for processing are satisfied, how data minimisation will be applied, how individuals' rights will be fulfilled and the appropriate security measures needed to keep the data secure and confidential.

Any concerns regarding the legal compliance of the project should be raised and addressed early on in the project life-cycle as it may surprise stakeholders that they cannot just collect and process personal data as they see fit. In which case, some technical solutions and designs may require adjustment in order to add legally required features and this is best done at the outset of the project. Remember, the aim of Privacy by Design.

3. Identify and assess privacy risks

The GDPR requires a risk assessment approach to identifying and assessing privacy threats and assessing compliance with the regulations. This assessment should be performed at the initial stages of the product or service life-cycle but it is an on-going process (as the project develops or enters service and matures, new risks may be identified and others may be obsolete). The PIA dove-tails nicely into standard project and software development lifecycles during the risk assessment phase so can be accommodated seamlessly into all projects that follow a common framework.

The best practice guidance takes a broad approach to identifying privacy risks, saying that organisations 'should identify any privacy risks to individuals, compliance risks and any related risks for the organisation; such as fines for non-compliance with legislation or reputational damage leading to loss of business'.

An important part of the traditional IT or security risk approach is assessing the likelihood and impact should an identified feared event occur and that standard risk assessment technique is based upon subject matter expertise and experience. This is important in practice, as the severity of the impact and the likelihood (the probability) of the risk occurring will influence the measures that a controller takes to mitigate the risk.

For example, risk counter measures should be proportional to the probability and the loss so a Controller will not be expected to implement expensive mitigation mechanisms if the probability of occurrence and the cost of loss are both deemed to be very low. This is where Subject Matter Expertise is vital as it is their experience that is drawn when evaluating the probability of risk through identified threats materialising.

Therefore an organisation should understand the importance of consultation with employees at all levels throughout the PIA process, and in particular when identifying privacy risks, to ensure that people with subject matter expertise in a relevant area are able to highlight risks and assess the likelihood and impact of the risk occurring.

4. Consider ways of addressing risks

Once privacy risks have been identified, the next step is to consider ways of addressing them. Consultation with appropriate specialists at this stage will help to identify potential and pragmatic solutions to the risks.

If possible it is often the optimum approach to avoid risks completely for example by not collecting certain types of personal data or by reducing the threat of disclosure to an acceptable level by using Pseudonymisation, redaction or implementing proactive robust security measures.

Assessing for GDPR Compliance

Once the organisation has established a baseline of readiness by addressing the issues that surfaced during the preceding gap analysis and PIA it can begin to start the iterative process of performing Data Protection Impact Assessments in order to ensure compliancy with the Regulation.

For those new to risk assessments and many SMB organizations are – even large ones – then the following sections will provide some guidance in performing a DPIA. Whether you are an experienced or a novice in risk assessment design the PIA\DPIA should be structured so that it can be a module easily inserted into the organizations project management or software development life-cycle. This is advisable so that future projects will have Privacy by Design and by Default built into them from conception and not bolted on later.

Whether the organisation chooses to use a PIA or a DPIA in the project life-cycle will come down to the element of risk as the GDPR states that a DPIA must be done, is mandatory, when processing is "likely to result in a high risk" and remember this is from the perspective of the rights and freedoms of the data subjects.

As we saw earlier the DPIA is a GDPR specific assessment with a focus on compliance hence it is imperative to take guidance from the GDPR articles (35) or from the Article 29 Working Party who issue guidelines and clarifications on the Articles and in particular on the DPIA.

Article 35(3) provides some examples of when processing is likely to result in high risk will include processing:

- based on automated decision-based processing, including profiling,
- processing on a large scale of special categories of data
- personal data relating to criminal convictions and offences; or

- a systematic monitoring of a publicly accessible area on a large scale.

However, the WP29 also clarifies the point that an organisation does not require to perform a DPIA – though it is still recommended – if the processing is not "likely to result in a high risk to the rights and freedoms of natural persons", or that they have prior permission from their DPA or the processing is similar/compatible with processing that they have permission for already or they have exemptions from the clause.

The Article 29 WP recommends carrying out a DPIA nonetheless as it is a useful tool to help data controllers comply with data protection laws. The WP29 guidelines also include some advice on recommended practice, whilst leaving the methodology up to the organisation. They suggest that every step of the DPIA process should be documented, and any decision not to conduct a DPIA should be supported by evidence of the reason for that decision.

The WP29 states that at a minimum the DPIA should include:

- a description of the envisaged processing operations and the purposes of the processing;
- an assessment of the necessity and proportionality of the processing;
- an assessment of the risks to the rights and freedoms of data subjects;
- the measures envisaged to:
  - address the risks; and
  - demonstrate compliance with the GDPR

Furthermore, WP29 recommends that the organisation publishes a redacted copy of the DPIA to help foster trust in their processing operations, and demonstrate accountability and transparency. They suggest that the published DPIA does not need to contain the whole assessment; it can consist of a summary of the main findings.

As a diligently undertaken PIA\DPIA can be a time consuming exercise it does not make sense to physically reproduce that effort for every identical or very similar project. The GDPR takes this into account and so permits a single assessment to address a set of similar processing operations that present similar levels of risks. As such, it is foreseeable that industry bodies may produce impact assessments for common processes. Further, privacy conscious processors may decide to complete impact assessments for the technology and services they are providing to controllers and may publish or advertise the redacted results as a value-add differentiator of service.

When working through the Privacy Impact Assessment and/or a Data Protection Impact Assessment try to keep in mind some essential privacy building blocks which will assist in providing a structured GDPR Readiness and Compliance framework:

1. Prepare for data security breaches

Construct and document clear policies based upon well-practiced procedures to ensure that those concerned can react quickly to any data breach and notify the regulators in time where required. Consider setting up a central breach management unit to collate, review and notify breaches, where appropriate.
Review and update the technical and organisational measures in light of the increased security obligations in the GDPR.

2. Establish a framework for accountability
Appoint a data protection officer, but only if required. Also ensure that there are clear policies in place to prove that the organization meets the required standards. Establish a culture of monitoring, reviewing and assessing the data processing procedures, aiming to satisfy the principles of minimization, transparency and purpose of data processing and retention of data, and building in safeguards. Ensure that relevant parties create and maintain records of the processing that are carrying out per controller or processor (unless exempt).

It is also advantageous to adapt the project and product development processes to include a privacy impact assessment to meet the goals of Privacy by Design and Default.
Check that the organisations relevant employees are trained to understand their obligations through an Awareness initiative. In addition also provide documented evidence of due diligence by producing an auditable privacy impact assessments. Further, this or a similar risk assessment will also need to be conducted to review and document any ongoing risky processing activities and the mitigation measures taken to address specific concerns.

3. Embrace privacy by design

Ensure that privacy is embedded into any new processing or product that is deployed through incorporating a standard PIA into the project or development plan. This enables a structured assessment and systematic validation of all future product or service initiatives. Implementing privacy by design can both demonstrate compliance and create competitive advantage through product/service differentiation.

4. Analyse the legal basis on which you use personal data

Consider what lawful basis is used for any data processing the organization undertakes. A common misconception is that organizations often assume that they need to obtain the consent of data subjects to process their data.
However, consent is just one of several legitimate ways of processing personal data (the exception being special category personal data) and may not be suitable as it can be readily withdrawn.
One alternative that is feasible if the organisation can show that they have a legitimate interest in processing personal data that is not in conflict with or overridden by the interests of the data subject, is the Legitimate Interest clause. There is also lawful processing allowed if the purpose of processing is fundamental to the contractual agreement, for example a health & fitness wearable wristband may require to send the personal health data collected to the cloud to be collated and analysed as that is fundamental to its purpose and contract however

the organisation or vendor may have to demonstrate that was the case as they will always bear the burden of proof.

If obtaining consent is the only legitimate method feasible, then it is up to the organisation to review the documents and forms of consent to ensure they are adequate and check that consents are freely given, specific, informed and require affirmative action.

5. Check your privacy notices and policies

The GDPR requires that information provided should be in clear and plain language. Therefore it is mandatory that policies should be transparent and easily accessible. Long winded and deliberately obfuscated documents using legalese will no longer be accepted so many organisations may have to update their existing privacy notices. Organisations should adopt the principle of transparency when drafting these documents and be fair, open and honest.

6. Bear in mind the rights of data subjects

Organisation should have processes and procedures in place and be proactively prepared for data subjects exercising their rights under the GDPR, such as the right to data portability and the right to erasure. If organisations must store personal data, consider the legitimate grounds for its retention – it will be their burden of proof to demonstrate that the legitimate grounds override the interests of the data subjects. Consider if individuals are likely to exercise their new rights and what that may mean for the operation in practical terms. Based on that analysis, set up technical and organizational measures and processes to capture, record and act on those requests and be capable of demonstrating that procedure to the regulators.

7. If you are a supplier of processing service to others, consider whether you have new obligations as a processor.

The GDPR imposes some new direct obligations on processors which will require a revision of strategy, policies, procedures and contracts. Processors are likely to find that their customers, the controllers, will wish to ensure that the processor services they contract are compatible with the enhanced requirements of the Regulation. Consider whether the contractual documentation is adequate and, for existing contracts, check who is responsible for later changes to the service as a result of foreseen or importantly any unforeseen changes in laws or regulations. If as a processor you subcontract data processing services to or from a third party, it is very important to determine and document the respective responsibilities.

8. Cross-border data transfers

For any international data transfers, including intra-group transfers, out with the EU it is mandatory to have a legitimate basis for transferring personal data to jurisdictions that are not recognised as having adequate data protection regulation for example the US. Therefore it is imperative that the organisation reviews any current transfer agreements or mechanisms as failure to comply could attract a fine of up to the greater of EUR20m and 4% of annual worldwide turnover, the consequences of non-compliance could be severe. Hence the organisation should consider if the current methods are legitimate and justified now and will continue to be so under the GDPR.
There are several legitimate ways to transfer data internationally and an organisation should consider implementing a "structural" transfer solution to justify their transfers. For larger organisations they may want to consider adopting binding corporate rules to facilitate intra-group transfers of data but for SMB that may not be feasible so they could consider codes of conduct, certification or arrange an ad hoc agreement with their regulator.

Chapter VII – Deriving Business Opportunities via Compliance

For many organizations GDPR will precipitate the need of a cultural shift, as well as providing technical and organisational challenges which they have never had to face before. For some it will not be easy to shift the focus of their attention to the rights of privacy for the individual as previously they paid only lip-service to privacy laws and directives. Now things have changed and they will have to embed *privacy by design and default*, into not only their products (goods and services), but into their very culture. GDPR compliance is not an option and it will demand a complete shift in the mindsets of executives, stakeholders, project managers and all the other employees that process individual data within an organization.

As an example of the sea shift required, if awareness training is competent then many operational support and product design teams will become all too aware of the importance of data privacy and the current relative shortfall from the required levels of protection that compliance demand. It should become clear to operational and technical teams the necessity for designing in privacy during design and implementation processes of new products and services.

There are many operational and design challenges and new processes that will be required to comply with the obligations of GDPR. However, most of these obligations are current burdens, which can be in the longer term advantageous and so should be viewed as an opportunity to bring about a cultural change in the way the organization approaches and respects the transparency of service, data security, privacy and ultimate the rights of individuals.

Bringing about such a seismic shift will be no easy task and to gain this benefit an organisation will need to envisage and execute a strategic approach to data governance, privacy and management.

So where can these advantages come from?

Big Data and data analytics are in the news and are prevalent throughout all the large data controllers and processors. However to optimise the benefits and have data analysis work at its true potential requires an abundance of clean quality data. One of the impediments to data analytics and machine learning is the shortage of quality data, and that is defined as data that is up-to-date; that's accurate; that's relevant; and when it comes to personal data, you need it to be lawful i.e. it has the consent of the individual that it relates too.

Not so long ago contact centres and marketing departments often measured their databases by the quantity of the records not by the quality. Hence there would often be erroneous claims made by naive marketing managers of them having hundreds of thousands of individual customer records in their CRM (Customer Relationship Database). Their belief of course was based upon a basic fact that the record count in the database table showed that number of supposedly unique customer records. Unfortunately when these database tables would be examined there would be not just duplicate or even quadruple records for the same customer, which contained conflicting information. Furthermore, there would be hundreds of records that were incomplete or contained just plain rubbish. It would not be unusual to find a table of say 200,000 individual records contained less than 20% genuine complete useable records and that was before you asked for evidence of the individuals consent.

However, data is valuable to an organisation hence the ubiquitous and overused term 'data is the new oil' but it is true in a sense that clean data means bigger profits for those that deal in it. Therefore, getting the organization to become more data aware and importantly data security aware will mean greater value is generated from the data assets.

Many of the data governance principles that would assist in refining data already exist under the present data protection directives: data minimisation; accuracy; storage limitation. There have been some extensions but no real changes in direction or philosophy so they haven't changed much in the GDPR. On the other hand what has changed is how organizations will be obliged to enforce data privacy and to do that they will be required to understand their data, categorise it and believe it or not actually know where it is. To do this they will need to build the discovery, categorisation and enforcement mechanisms that under GDPR have changed dramatically.

For European organisations or those with an establishment in Europe compliance with GDPR is not optional they will need to comply or go bust. However for non-European organisations that do not currently offer goods or services to the European market or monitor European resident's compliance is unnecessary. However, the internet is a global marketplace and the EU single market commands a combined population of 522 million with an average GDP of $36,000 per person and a combined GDP of $19 Trillion.

Therefore, doing business in the European Economic Area (EEA) is a very attractive proposition but does the GDPR make that infeasible for non-European SMB organizations?

There are several ways that US entities can in addition to the cost and time savings mentioned above, gain a commercial advantage from becoming GDPR compliant. For example although not relevant to the US, GDPR compliance not only opens up the EEA and its vast affluent consumer base to foreign organisations, it can serve as a competitive advantage in the US and other marketplaces by displaying a high standard of organizational competency.

Displaying competency and compliance with the GDPR is the opportunity to demonstrate, data governance excellence, via adherence to this more exacting and stringent data privacy regulations than required under US law. There will be opportunities to obtain certifications and become accredited GDPR compliant service provider. Certification engenders confidence and trust in the organization, and in this international marketplace provides the customer with a reference as to the organisations competency. Moreover the customer will also benefit from the many processes that GDPR stipulates in order to enhance individual data security and privacy such as the principles of transparency, privacy, and security with respect to the vendor's treatment of the customer's data.

Customer companies, the small business controllers, are increasingly seeking to out-source their obligations and regulatory requirements of their own State upon their vendor. Controllers that take this strategy and deal with vendors that comply with GDPR can do so with confidence.

GDPR Enforcement

As part of that increased transparency companies will need to tell their customers what purposes they'll be using their data for, and how long they will keep it for at the time that they collect the data.

The regulations of course apply to everyone so there is no competitive advantage to be gained there. However the point here will be not whether an organization has to grudgingly comply but rather how well and diligently they embrace the regulations.

Many organizations merely paid lip-service to the Data Protection Directives – some because they couldn't be bothered and never saw the incentive - as they were highly unlikely to be caught. Others because even though they knew they would be under the spotlight determined that the fines were so paltry as to be only a minor irritant hardly worthy of even trying to subvert the letter of the law.

The GDPR should change this but not drastically. In the former group those that believe themselves to fly under the radar are likely to continue in their own unregulated ways – until something bad happens to them. The latter group are the ones that will now know they must comply as there is nothing like a fine of 4% of worldwide turnover to concentrate the mind and focus the business practices on the spirit of the law.

However for both groups becoming compliant with the GDPR is beneficial as it encourages competent data governance and management. Data governance in turn demands diligent and effective Records Management and this will have an impact on an organisation way beyond the data protection regulations such as in:

- Accurate customer records
- effective customer interactions
- reduced storage costs
- more efficient data searches
- cleaner data for analytics
- less wasteful marketing campaigns
- lower security risks
- lower risks of regulatory penalties

For many organizations that shudder at the thought of the additional requirements for budget and resources there is also the possibility to simply minimize the risk through a coherent strategy of data minimization and protection. By minimizing the amounts of personal data an organization holds to the bare minimum greatly reduces the risk footprint. Furthermore, if the residual data can then be encrypted or otherwise secured robustly then the compliancy risks can also be proportionately reduced. For many organizations the starting point should be to review the data being collected and held and asking some basic questions, why do I need this data … How can I secure it?

The GDPR's emphasis on data security

The GDPR retains and expands upon the principles of security that are already in force under the current directive. In a similar manner to the directive GDPR does not stipulate how an organization must secure their data they just require *"appropriate technical and organisational measures"*. Now of course these appropriate measures vary greatly dependent on the organisation and the purpose for which it processes personal data. Therefore the GDPR requires than an organization takes a risk based approach to identifying there data assets, the opportunities and the threats whilst *"taking into account the state-of-the-art, the cost of implementation and the nature, scope, context and purpose of processing as well as the risk of varying likelihood and severity"*.

Therefore it is really up to the organization to show due diligence in conducting a competent risk assessment either through a Privacy Impact Assessment or for larger organizations and those dealing in any sensitive category personal data - through a Data Protection Impact Assessment (DPIA). (We discuss the difference between a Privacy Impact Assessment and the GDPR required DPIA in a later section.)

The onus is therefore on the organization to put in place sufficient security measures to ensure the privacy, integrity and confidentiality of the personal data they have in their possession.

For many risk-averse organizations the incentive to find the budgets and resources to implement sufficient security measures are clearly set out in the range of available penalties. Fines of 4% of global turnover provides quite an incentive to get your data governance act together, and have GDPR compliance high up on that Risk Register.

Other more risk tolerant organizations that are currently more cavalier in their attitudes and operations towards the directives must not sleepwalk into the spring of 2018 as the GDPR authorities will have both eyes fully open and may even be looking for a few convenient small to midsized miscreants to make an example.

If an organization insists upon a risky strategy of non-compliance as part of their overall strategic operational plan, then they must consider the reputational, financial and business risk that they are undertaking.

At first sight the GDPR just becomes a simple regulatory pressure on companies to respect the privacy of the individual. But for those organizations who can demonstrate, high levels of data governance and data security, there may well be benefits through reputational enhancement.

However, the challenges to GDPR are real and for most unprepared organizations they will be daunting. One of the most challenging may be just getting the awareness that the new regulation has a far wider territorial scope, which will include non-European organizations that provide goods or services aimed at the European market or monitor the behaviour of EU residents. There are some other interesting challenges which include the potential requirement of a Data Protection Officer, and the recommendations of a Data Impact Privacy Assessments being introduced into an amended privacy program for larger organisations or those that process large quantities of special category personal data.

However, there are 4 key benefits that can be derived through diligent efforts to pursue GDPR. Indeed the Regulation itself offers benefits compared to the current data protection scheme in place in Europe and it removes many of the current bugbears that organizations come across.

Simplified Access to the European Economic Area (Single Market)

Harmonizing of Organizational Processes and Procedures

A commonly overlooked benefit for predominantly large organizations with an established footprint across several EU Member States is that the quest for compliance to a single Regulation will in effect produce a common set of operational procedures across the whole organization. By extension this benefit also applies to SMB or other Enterprise organisations as they too will need to perform the same basic procedures and implement the same tactics and mechanisms to mitigate risk and achieve compliance and ergo produce common operational procedures. Therefore compliance to the GDPR should lead to a more coherent and compatible operational workflows and procedures across Controllers and Processors, leading to potentially a standardisation of service and contracts.

Harmonization of EU privacy laws

Currently under the existing directive a major issue for organizations operating in Europe and the largest source of complaints is that they have to monitor and comply with the laws of 28 different Member States. For smaller organizations such as SMB this is a significant obstacle in their path to opening up new business channels as the administration burden can be crippling. The reason that this administrative muddle came about was that the Data Protection Directive 95/46/EC provides only a framework for EU countries to develop and maintain their own privacy rules and regulations. This resulted in the current data privacy laws essentially being a patchwork of different laws from various Member States. This disparity in the regulations, which often leads to uncertainty for businesses and their EU-based clients, as well as substantial costs associated with compliance efforts.

GDPR however rather than being a Directive is a Regulation, which has binding legal force throughout every Member State and enters into force on a set date in all the Member States. Therefore, except for some provisions for employment and law enforcement the regulations are a uniform set of data privacy regulations implemented across all Member States. This has the benefit of greatly simplifying regulations and reduces risk by following a uniform set of rules that apply to the entire European Union.

Lead authority one-stop shop

As with the aim for harmonisation of data privacy laws, the goals of the 'One-Stop-Shop' mechanism is to simplify access to Regulators and provide a single Data Protection Authority touch-point for organisations who have multiple establishments in several EU Member States. One of the key elements of the GDPR was to remove the conflict between DPAs where sometimes conflicting information and interpretations of the Directive would be supplied to an organisation with a presence across Member States. It was hoped that it would resolve this confusion and provide unified supervision and interpretation of the law by providing one lead authority to companies with a presence in more than one Member State.

Unfortunately, despite the best intentions the mechanism is in fact more complicated than many had anticipated. Where the 'One-Stop-Shop' mechanism does apply, there are complex cooperation and coordination procedures for DPAs as it distinguishes between cross-border and domestic processing.

In order to enable individuals to have their cases dealt with locally, the GDPR contains a detailed hierarchal regime with a Lead Authority and Concerned Authorities working together. However, it seems most organisations would have preferred a system where one single privacy regulator has exclusive competence over regulation. Instead the One-Stop-Shop mechanism under the GDPR allows organisations to deal with one "lead authority", which is the DPA in the State of the organisation's main establishment.

The way that it works is the Lead Authority acts as a mediator or adjudicator and a single point of contact for the organisation. However the individual state data protection authorities will still have the ability to investigate and enforce data protection issues if a complaint is directed to them. The difference is that they must notify the lead authority of its intention to investigate or take action.

The lead authority will then have three weeks to determine whether it wishes to intervene and operate in a joint manner. While there are other nuances and exceptions, as a whole, GDPR's designation of a lead authority has the potential to effectively promote various countries to work together on enforcement and investigation matters in a predictable and efficient manner, allowing companies to focus time, energy, and resources on dealing with one regulator.

Data breach reporting

The current EU Directive does not contain a general data breach-reporting obligation. Rather, data breach reporting requirements are predetermined by each member country. GDPR introduces a general but stringent obligation to report data breaches to both Controllers and Processors though the clauses differ. GDPR also states that the breached entity must, without undue delay, notify the supervisory authority within 72 hours of becoming aware of personal data breach that has led to a compromise of confidentiality or other significant risk to the individual.

However far from being a burden the new GDPR's breach notification requirement may be advantageous to many organisations. This is due to an organisation now being freed from the burden of recording and managing the disparity between breach reporting regulations in each Member State. As a result, contract negotiation over data breach provisions can be streamlined by virtue of the vendor company, providing detailed data breach reporting obligation provisions in their standard contracts as a component of GDPR compliance. Furthermore, having to report to only one supervisory authority saves time and energy for in-house counsel, particularly for smaller in-house departments. GDPR allows companies to have one all-encompassing EU data breach response plan.

Chapter VIII - Brexit and the GDPR

On 23 June 2016 the UK held a referendum to decide whether or not to remain in the EU and the majority voted to leave. This decision came as a shock as opinion polls had leading up to the Referendum indicated a comfortable win for those that wished to remain. Indeed the UK voted to leave the EU only two months after the European Parliament voted on the new *EU General Data Protection Regulation* (GDPR). This naturally has generated much uncertainty, as many organisations based in the UK or with UK subsidiaries were preparing to comply with the GDPR and they are now left in a flux wondering what they should do, especially with regard to transfers of personal data between the remaining 27 EU countries and the UK after Brexit.

Following the Referendum, the UK government has stated its intention to give notice to leave the EU under Article 50 of the Treaty on European Union on the 29th of March 2017. However the process of leaving the EU is a long and convoluted so the UK would then expect to leave on withdrawal terms being agreed or by the expiry of two years from giving notice, so by end March 2019.

Due to the complications of agreeing withdrawal terms and importantly establishing agreeable terms for the future relationship between the parties it is highly likely that GDPR will come into force in May 2018 before the UK negotiates their exit for the EU.

This of course leaves organisations in the UK or with UK relationships in a quandary as they will need to comply with GDPR as of the accepted date of 26th May 2018 but for how long? The dilemma is that these organisations may have to go through extensive cost and effort to put into place compliancy measures only for the UK to ditch the GDPR a few months later.

Currently, in the lead up to the enforcement date of GDPR and several months after the activation of Article 50 – the indication of the UK's intention to leave the EU, there has been no firm advice from the UK Government regards its position albeit they have made indications that GDPR or something closely resembling it would remain. To compound the issue the UK Government also plans to review all legislation adopted by the Great Repeal Act following departure from the EU to assess what, if any, changes to it should be made. This will include GDPR.

The problem is that GDPR in its entirety is unlikely to remain as it has too many Articles that reference Member States and EU organizations and other EU regulations and Directives. For example, GDPR provisions in relation to the EDPB, cooperation and enforcement between member states and the consistency mechanism would need careful consideration and some adjustment to work effectively if the UK were outside the EU. Therefore a new UK mirror version of GDPR is likely to be redrafted and adopted.

Any proposed tinkering and customisation of GDPR provisions for the UK would have to take account of the extra territorial reach of GDPR, and of the impact of data transfer rules. The UK Government and the ICO will need to ensure UK businesses have a clear idea of the requirements with which they will need to comply to minimise confusion and maximise efficiency.

The data transfer rules is very problematic as currently under the GDPR, transfers of personal data to outside the EEA can only be made lawfully in certain limited circumstances. As long as the UK remains a member of the EU, it remains within the EEA. In the event that the UK leaves the EU, it ceases to be within the EEA. That is a binary choice the UK is either in or out of the EEA. Therefore, regardless of whether or not it has adopted GDPR, the UK would no longer be part of the EU safe zone for personal data. Personal data transfers to the UK from within the EEA would no longer carry automatic adequate safeguard. There is also an addition often overlooked issue of data transfers from other global regions to the UK which are compliant based on the UK being within the EU or EEA, as these transfers may no longer be considered legitimate.

Whether or not the UK is within or outside the EU, UK businesses and organisations may still be subject to GDPR from 25 May 2018, if they monitor the behaviour of, or offer goods and services to, citizens in the EU from the UK just as GDPR jurisdiction extends to other non-European organizations. Therefore the question as to whether UK based organisations require to be compliant with the GDPR is rather moot, if they want to do business in the EU that entails processing personal data of EU citizens then they will have to demonstrate like organisations from every other non-European country that they are GDPR compliant.

If the UK ceases to be within the EEA once it leaves the EU, personal data transfers to the UK – even intra-group – will be considered as transfers out with the EU and hence come under the strict clauses regulation such activity. This will cause issues with GDPR compliant organisations in the EEA with a UK presence as they will need to identify which systems and servers are located in the UK. In addition they will need to identify which entities and operations transfer personal data to the UK and conversely where UK operations access personal data held elsewhere in the EEA.

As a result if the UK leaves the EU then it is likely that new adequate safeguard measures may need to be put in place for all these scenarios, such as European Model Clauses.

Of course if the UK joins the EEA, the UK would have to adopt the GDPR. In principle, the UK might leave the EU and join the EEA, which currently includes all the EU Member States, plus Iceland, Liechtenstein and Norway. Joining the EEA would enable the UK to be part of the EU Single Market but the UK would have to comply with relevant EU laws relating to the four freedoms of the EU Single Market, including the GDPR. However, since in it appears that the UK is against what is perceived as a continuing loss of sovereignty and in particular interference by the Court of Human Rights and the free movement of people, in practice, it appears rather unlikely that the UK would decide to join the EEA.

Another possible Brexit scenario that has been suggested is that the UK would try to obtain an "adequacy decision" from the Commission for its own data protection laws, to demonstrate that the UK shares the same high regard for citizen's privacy rights. In this case, the UK would apply for an "adequacy decision" for its *own legislation*, so that businesses could freely transfer personal data from the EU to the UK.

Unfortunately, Jan Philipp Albrecht, the European Parliament rapporteur of the GDPR, seemed to find this unlikely as there would be "less safeguards for intelligence services [in the UK] than in the [United States]", the US fails the adequacy requirements due to the powers of intelligence services go beyond what is necessary and proportionate.

Regardless of whether the UK was or was not treated as a special case in a 'adequacy decision' it would still take several years to push through which creates a gap between Brexit and any Free Trade Agreement (FTA). Consequently there is currently much activity in finding a solution in bridging this gap by means of a transitional agreement.

In conclusion and to cut a long answer short UK organisations or organizations with UK subsidiaries need to prepare for the GDPR regardless of any future FTA or transitional agreements. This is simply because it is likely that the GDPR will apply to them in May 2018 which will be before the UK actually leaves the EU. (The Gap)

In addition it also appears likely that either the UK will adopt the GDPR itself in the end, or at least a very similar data protection law in order to secure the legitimate transfer of personal data with the EU.

Furthermore, there will be many instances where the GDPR will apply to UK organisations long after Brexit because organisations will have establishments in the EU/EEA. Additionally, many UK organisations will wish to follow GDPR compliance because processing of personal data of EU/EEA residents is related to the offering of goods or services to such individuals or the monitoring of their behaviour and they will want to be part of that vast marketplace of over 500 million affluent potential customers and with a combined GDP of $19 Trillion dollars. Seriously, no business will intentionally ostracize themselves from a market of that size and potential.

Part III – A Review of the GDPR Articles

Study of the GDPR Articles

After over four years of deliberation, debate and drafting, the new EU data protection framework was adopted on 8 April 2016. It takes the form of a Regulation – the General Data Protection Regulation (GDPR).

The GDPR will replace the current Data Protection Directive and will be directly applicable in all Member States from the 25 May 2018. However, as it contains some onerous obligations, many of which will take time to prepare for, the GDPR will likely have an immediate impact. Although the regulation took four years of discussion there has always been a desire to get the GDPR agreed quickly, even if that meant that some of the detail was left for later consideration. One of the chief drivers for early agreement was the desire to harmonize the disparate laws and regulations across the 28 member states.

The GDPR introduces some important changes to the current directive and the Article 29 Working Party has been working with organization to help them adjust to the new regulatory obligations.

One of the most important changes to the Directive is the territorial scope of GDPR as the regulation now catches data controllers and processors outside the EU whose processing activities relate to the offering of goods or services (even if for free) to, or monitoring the behaviour of, EU data subjects (within the EU). Furthermore many of these non-European organizations will need to appoint a representative that is based in the EU.

The GDPR is a set of 11 Chapters containing 99 articles that are accompanied by Recitals and these provide some more information, examples and some helpful guidance. For example in the case of "Offering goods or services" we can read in the Recitals that it is more than mere access to a website or email address, but might be evidenced by use of language or currency generally used in one or more Member States with the possibility of ordering goods/services there, and/or mentioning customers or users who are in EU.

"Monitoring of behaviour" will occur, for example, where individuals are tracked on the internet by techniques which apply a profile to enable decisions to be made/predict personal preferences, etc.

This means in practice that a company outside the EU which is targeting consumers in the EU will be subject to the GDPR. This is not the case currently.

Chapter IX – GDPR Articles and Recitals

The following Chapters relate to the 11 Chapter of the General Data Protection Regulation and their respective Articles and Recitals.

Chapter 1 – General Provisions

What we will cover in this Chapter are the following articles;

Article 1: Subject matter and objectives
Article 2: Material scope
Article 3: Territorial scope
Article 4: Definitions

Defining the subject matter and objectives

The objectives of the GDPR are;

Article 1 - Aims and objectives of the law

EU data protection law aims to govern the processing of personal data and to ensure that such processing is fair and lawful. It is also designed to give effect to the fundamental right to privacy, enshrined in Art.7 of the CFR and Art. 8 of the ECHR.

The GDPR is intended to:

- protect the fundamental rights and freedoms of data subjects;
- enable the free movement of personal data within the EU;
- contribute to economic and social progress and trade;
- address the processing of personal data in the light of technological progress; and
- Harmonise data protection laws across the EU.

The only difference between the Data Protection Directive currently in place and the GDPR is the determination to 'Harmonise data protection laws across the EU' and bring in a regulation that applies across all Member States

It is at this point we need to remind ourselves of the difference between an EU Directive and a Regulation. In EU terms there are two main types of legislation:

- Directives – A directive is a legal act of the European Union, which requires member states to achieve a particular result without dictating the means of achieving that result. It can be distinguished from regulations which are self-executing and do not require any implementing measures.
    - Requires individual implementation in each member state
    - Implemented by the creation of national laws approved by the parliaments of each member state
    - The Data Protection Directive 95/46/EC is a directive
    - The UK law DPA (Data Protection Act 1998) is an implementation of the directive DPD 95/46/EC into UK law.
- Regulation - A regulation is a legal act of the European Union that becomes immediately enforceable as law in all member states simultaneously. Regulations can be distinguished from directives which, at least in principle, need to be transposed into national law.
    - Immediately applicable in each EU member state
    - Requires no local implementation legislation
    - EU GDPR is a regulation (This Regulation shall be binding in its entirety in all member states)*

*Albeit there are allowances for each Member State to make changes in certain areas for provisions related to specific areas such as Employment Law and Law Enforcement and National Security.

Furthermore the EU GDPR was entered into force on 24th of May 2016 and applies on 25th of May 2018.

Data to which the law applies

"The law protects the personal data of natural persons, but does not apply to data of deceased persons. However, Member States may provide for rules regarding the processing of data of deceased persons."

The GDPR clarifies that EU data protection law does not apply to the data of deceased persons. Previously under the Data Protection Directive this was not clear and consequently the Member States have addressed it differently.

Therefore, EU data protection law applies to personal data of natural person – a living individual. In addition under the GDPR a natural person has rights associated with:

- The protection of personal data
- The protection of the processing of personal data
- The unrestricted movement of personal data within the EU

Article 2 – Material Scope

Under the article covering the material scope of the GDPR the stipulation that the regulation is technology neutral is made.

Systems to which the law applies

"EU data protection law only applies to personal data that are processed in the context of: automated systems (e.g., any electronic database or computerised filing system); or relevant filing systems"

This is compatible with the current DPD so there is no change with regards the type of technology or systems which apply to GDPR.

However, in the GDPR it expands on a definition for what it regards is a relevant filing system, the GDPR defines it as being:

'A "relevant filing system" is any structured set of personal data that can be searched or accessed by reference to relevant criteria (e.g., name, ID number, telephone number, etc.). For example, a filing cabinet containing HR records arranged in alphabetical order of employee names would be a relevant filing system. An unstructured box of hard copy case files arranged by year only (and not labelled by name or any other identifier specific to any individual) would not be a relevant filing system. Data contained in the documents within that box would fall outside the scope of EU data protection law, until such time as those data are structured or processed for another purpose.'

Therefore we can consider that under the article 2 Material Scope GDPR covers:

- Personal data that is processed wholly or partially by automated means
- Personal data that is part of a filing system or is intended to be

Persons to whom the law applies

EU data protection law applies across all sectors to all organisations that are subject to the law.

"The GDPR applies to natural and legal persons, public authorities, agencies and other bodies which process personal data."

Again this is wholly compatible with the DPD although one expansion is that Data Processors have different levels and obligations for compliance as we will see later.

Exclusions and exemptions

EU data protection law explicitly excludes and exempts certain activities from its scope.

The following processing is outside the scope of the GDPR:

- *any activity outside the scope of EU law (e.g., activities of a Member State in relation to national criminal law);*
- *any activity performed by Member States when carrying out activities in relation to the common foreign and security policy of the EU;*
- *any activity performed by a natural person in the course of a purely personal or household activity;*
- *any processing by the EU itself; and*
- *Any activities performed by national authorities for the purposes of prevention, investigation, detection or prosecution of criminal offences, or performance of judicial functions.*

The GDPR exclude a number of activities that, while they constitute the processing of personal data, are outside the scope of EU data protection law. One notable area is where the GDPR has extended the groups that they consider exempt from the regulations by adding any activities performed by national authorities for the purposes of law enforcement which they list as the prevention, investigation, detection or prosecution of criminal offences, or performance of judicial functions. This means that processing performed by national police forces and courts will not be subject to the GDPR.

An area that did need clarification was over the exemption regarding 'Household activity' which was addressed by the CJEU. They determined that the "household purposes" exemption is strictly limited to purely personal activities for example any personal correspondence or personal use of social networking services. However, confusion may arise when activities, which are partly personal and partly professional (e.g., sending correspondence that includes both social content and business-related content) as the activity then does not benefit from this exemption.

Hence, organisations that provide services to individuals for such purposes (e.g., social network providers) do not benefit from this exemption.

Article – 3 Territorial Scope

The GDPR has extended its territorial scope to apply to all organisations that are established in the EU. However, for organisations established outside the EU, the GDPR may or may not apply, depending on the circumstances. However as the GDPR doesn't necessarily apply to every organization it is essential in establishing whether the GDPR applies to an organisation.

Currently under the Directive an organisation that falls under the scope of the regulations requires some sort of connection with the EU (e.g., an establishment or "means of processing" in the EU) the GDPR however has expanded that reach and now can apply to an organisation that has neither of these things. Instead, the GDPR focuses on the question of whether an organisation markets its products in the EU.

This can be a significant change for organisations that are not currently subject to the Directive, but that either offer goods or services to EU residents or monitor their behaviour; these changes are likely to lead to significant new compliance obligations and additional costs under the GDPR.

Establishment

One potential area for confusion is that organisations are subject to EU data protection law if they have an establishment in the EU. However the term 'Establishment' is not clearly defined. The GDPR implies it to mean "effective and real exercise of activity through stable arrangements".

If that is the correct interpretation then the GDPR applies to organisations that:

- are established in one or more Member State(s); and
- Process personal data (either as controller, processor, or both or regardless of whether or not the processing takes place in the EU) in the context of that establishment.

What that means is that just because you have an office established in the EU does not necessarily mean that you will come under GDPR. Therefore an organization may have several offices throughout the EU but so long as it does not process or transfer EU residents' personal data out with the EU it may not require being GDPR compliant. The key point being that the legal status of the organization's presence is determined by the personal data processing activities of that organization not its physical presence.

However we need to clarify that point as an organisation may have for example an office in the EU and not process any personal data from that EU office but they would still be subject to GDPR if they processed EU subjects personal data elsewhere out with the EU. This is because under GDPR a Data Controller or Data Processor must comply with GDPR regardless of where the processing takes place. Processing is very loosely termed to mean anything you do to personal data including the acts of collecting or storing the personal data, just handling the data is considered processing.

The GDPR articles attempt to clarify the term activities and the territorial scope by saying that:

The GDPR applies to organisations established outside the EU if they (either as controller or processor) process the personal data of EU residents when offering them goods or services (whether or not in return for payment). The question of what constitutes "offering" goods or services to EU residents is determined on a case-by-case basis:

- *Mere website accessibility of a service in the EU is not sufficient to trigger application of the GDPR.*
- *Factors such as offering a service in the languages or currencies used in a Member State (if not also used in the*

third country), or mentioning customers or users in a Member State may trigger application of the GDPR.

However GDPR doesn't just apply to organizations which *process the personal data of EU residents when offering them goods or services,* it also allies to those organizations that monitor the activities of EU residents and this is extremely relevant to internet technology organizations that track and harvest personal user data with or without their consent.

Monitoring of EU residents

Bringing the GDPR up to date so that it has relevance in today's internet centric world has required that the EU data protection law may apply to organizations that monitor the behaviour of EU residents.

The GDPR applies to organisations established outside the EU if they (whether as controller or processor) monitor the behaviour of EU residents (to the extent that such behaviour takes place in the EU). The question of what constitutes "monitoring" is determined on a case-by-case basis:

- *"monitoring" may include tracking an EU resident on the internet; and*
- *"Monitoring" may also include the use of data processing techniques to profile individuals, their behaviours or their attitudes (e.g., in order to analyse or predict personal preferences).*

For any organisation that is already monitoring the behaviour of EU residents either through an establishment in the EU or a "means of processing" in the EU, and are compliant with the current DPD obligations then these changes will require minimal operational review. For organisations that are not currently subject or complying to the Directive but are or intend to monitor the behaviour of EU residents, these changes mean that an organisation is subject to the full range of compliance obligations under the GDPR, in relation to the relevant processing activities.

Article 4 – Definitions

Article 4 is a critical document as it defines many of the important terms and roles within GDPR. In the introduction to this book we explained what some of the key roles were and how they applied today under the DPD. GDPR only makes a few changes to the definitions but we should be clear with regards how each role or activity is defined especially is we are new to the existing DPD as many of these terms will be confusing.

The GDPR defines the key roles and activities as being:

Personal data

This definition is critical because EU data protection law only applies to personal data. Information that does not fall within the definition of "personal data" is not subject to EU data protection law.

"Personal data" means any information relating to an identified or identifiable natural person ("data subject"); an identifiable person is one who can be identified, directly or indirectly, in particular by reference to an identifier such as a name, an identification number, location data, online identifier or to one or more factors specific to the physical, physiological, genetic, mental, economic, cultural or social identity of that person.

For most parts the definition of Personal Data remains unchanged but with a few additional special categories added to modernise the regulations such as genetic, biometric and location data. This may be problematic for some organisations, as the explicit inclusion of location data, online identifiers and genetic data within the definition of "personal data" may result in additional compliance obligations (e.g., for online advertising businesses, many types of cookies become personal data under the GDPR, because those cookies constitute "online identifiers"). Furthermore, organizations that collect location data, which is common in mobile apps, will find themselves with compliance obligations therefore they may wish to audit what personal data their mobile apps or systems are collecting and how they are processing this data as part of a compliance audit.

Sensitive Personal Data

Sensitive Personal Data are special categories of personal data that are subject to additional protections. In general, organisations require stronger grounds to process Sensitive Personal Data than they require to process "regular" personal data.

"Sensitive Personal Data" are personal data, revealing racial or ethnic origin, political opinions, religious or philosophical beliefs, trade-union membership; data concerning health or sex life and sexual orientation; genetic data or biometric data. Data relating to criminal offences and convictions are addressed separately (as criminal law lies outside the EU's legislative competence).

For most organisations, the concept of "Sensitive Personal Data" remains unchanged so they will not need to make any significant changes to their working practices. As for organisations that process genetic or biometric data, those data are now expressly categorised as "Sensitive Personal Data", and will therefore be subject to additional protections and restrictions. Therefore organizations that do collect genetic or biometric data then they will need to audit their processes to ensure they are GDPR compliant.

One way to ensure that the organization does not fall under the regulatory control of GDPR with regards personal data is to anonymized any person data that is collected. The EU GDPR takes two approaches to organizations collecting or holding personal data that has been anonymized or pseudoanonymized.

Anonymous data

Some sets of data can be amended in such a way that no individuals can be identified from those data (whether directly or indirectly) by any means or by any person. Ensuring that there is no way in which individuals can be identified is a technically complex task.

The GDPR does not apply to data that are rendered anonymous in such a way that individuals cannot be identified from the data.

As a result, personal data that are fully anonomised (i.e., data from which no individuals can be identified) are exempt from both the Directive and the GDPR.

Pseudonymous data

Some sets of data can be amended in such a way that no individuals can be identified from those data (whether directly or indirectly) without a "key" that allows the data to be re-identified. A good example of pseudonymous data is coded data sets used in clinical trials.

Pseudonymous data are still treated as personal data because they enable the identification of individuals (albeit via a key). However, provided that the "key" that enables re-identification of individuals is kept separate and secure, the risks associated with pseudonymous data are likely to be lower, and so the levels of protection required for those data are likely to be lower.

Pseudonymisation of data provides advantages. It can allow organisations to satisfy their obligations of "privacy by design" and "privacy by default" and it may be used to justify processing that would otherwise be deemed "incompatible" with the purposes for which the data were originally collected In addition, the GDPR explicitly encourages organisations to consider Pseudo-anonomised as a security measure.

Processing

The term "processing" is very broad. It essentially means anything that is done to, or with, personal data (including simply collecting, storing or deleting those data). This definition is significant because it clarifies the fact that EU data protection law is likely to apply wherever an organisation does anything that involves or affects personal data.

"Processing" means any operation or set of operations performed upon personal data or sets of personal data, whether or not by automated means, such as collection, recording, organisation, structuring, storage, adaptation or alteration, retrieval, consultation, use, disclosure by transmission, dissemination or otherwise making available, alignment or combination, restriction, erasure or destruction.

Data Controller

Under the Directive, the term "controller" has particular importance because compliance obligations under EU data protection law are primarily imposed on controllers. Under the GDPR, controllers still bear the primary responsibility for compliance, although processors also have direct compliance obligations under the GDPR.

"Controller" means the natural or legal person, public authority, agency or any other body which alone or jointly with others determines the purposes and means of the processing of personal data; where the purposes and means of processing are determined by EU or Member State laws, the controller (or the criteria for nominating the controller) may be designated by those laws.

Data Processor

The term "processor" refers to any entity that processes personal data under the controller's instructions (e.g., many service providers are processors).

"Processor" means a natural or legal person, public authority, agency or any other body which processes personal data on behalf of the controller.

Consent

The concept of "consent" is foundational to EU data protection law. In general, the validly obtained consent of the data subject will permit almost any type of processing activity, including Cross-Border Data Transfers.

"The consent of the data subject" means any freely given, specific, informed and unambiguous indication of his or her wishes by which the data subject, either by a statement or by a clear affirmative action, signifies agreement to personal data relating to them being processed.

The GDPR makes it considerably harder for organisations to obtain valid consent from data subjects for organisations that rely on consent for their business activities, the processes by which they obtain consent will need to be reviewed and revised to meet the requirements of the GDPR.

Data breaches

The term "data breach" is commonly used to refer to the scenario in which a third party gains unauthorised access to data, including personal data.

"Data breach" means a breach of security leading to the accidental or unlawful destruction, loss, alteration, unauthorised disclosure of, or access to, personal data transmitted, stored or otherwise processed.

Although the GDPR introduces a formal definition that is not provided in the Directive, the concept of a data breach does not materially change.

Data concerning health

The idea that health data should be treated as Sensitive Personal Data is well-established, and is also reflected in the laws of a number of jurisdictions outside the EU.

"Data concerning health" means personal data relating to the physical or mental health of an individual, including the provision of health care services, which reveal information about his or her health status. It expressly covers both physical and mental health.

The GDPR substantially increases the types of data that are included in the definition of "data concerning health". However, in practical terms, organisations already treat many of these types of data as "data concerning health", so these amendments to the formal definition are unlikely to result in wholesale changes in practice.

Organisations across the EU and beyond have been frustrated by the increasing lack of harmonisation across the Member States hence the GDPR.

Chapter II - Principles

In this chapter we will learn about articles 5 to 11 of the EU GDPR and what each article covers:

Article 5: Principles relating to personal data processing
Article 6: Lawfulness of processing
Article 7: Conditions for consent
Article 8: Conditions applicable to child's consent in relation to information society services
Article 9: Processing of special categories of personal data
Article 10: Processing of data relating to criminal convictions and offences
Article 11: Processing which does not require identification

The principles of articles 5 & 6 refer to transparency and data minimization as well as ensuring that organizations are able to satisfy the Data Protection Principles (and if no exemption or derogation applies) then such processing will be considered unlawful. It is therefore necessary for organizations to understand the principles of data protection and their underlying obligations set out in the GDPR.

Many non-EU organisations collect personal data and then later decide the purposes for which they wish to use those data. The Directive does not permit this approach, and the GDPR tightens the restrictions further, stating that organisations should not collect data that are not necessary for a specified purpose that has been notified to data subjects.

Organisations must ensure that, in relation to all processing activities by default, they process only the minimum amount of personal data necessary to achieve their lawful processing purposes. For example, in connection with an online service, a business must not collect personal data (e.g., contact details) that are not strictly necessary in connection with the provision of that service, unless the data subject chooses to provide those personal data. This is likely to require many businesses to re-think their data processing activities from the ground up.

Each organisation should carefully consider the extent to which it will need to amend its existing data collection practices in order to comply with these restrictions.

Article – 5 Fair, lawful and transparent processing

Fair, lawful and transparent processing

The requirement to process personal data fairly and lawfully is extensive. It includes, for example, an obligation to tell data subjects what their personal data will be used for.

Personal data must be processed lawfully, fairly and in a transparent manner in relation to the data subject.

This change imposes an additional compliance burden on organisations (albeit one that is implied under the Directive). It requires that organisations take additional care when designing and implementing data processing activities.

The purpose limitation principle

In summary, the purpose limitation principle states that personal data collected for one purpose should not be used for a new, incompatible, purpose.

Personal data may only be collected for specified, explicit and legitimate purposes and must not be further processed in a manner that is incompatible with those purposes. (Further processing of personal data for archiving purposes in the public interest, or scientific and historical research purposes or statistical purposes, in accordance with Art.89(1), is permitted

The GDPR brings limited changes to the principle of purpose limitation. Further processing of personal data for archiving, scientific, historical or statistical purposes is still permitted, but is subject to the additional safeguards provided in Art.89 of the GDPR.

Data minimisation

The principle of data minimisation is essentially the idea that, subject to limited exceptions, an organisation should only process the personal data that it actually needs to process in order to achieve its processing purposes

Personal data must be adequate, relevant and limited to what is necessary in relation to the purposes for which those data are processed.

The obligation to ensure that personal data are not excessive is replaced by a more restrictive obligation to ensure that personal data are "limited to what is necessary". Organisations will need to carefully review their data processing operations to consider whether they process any personal data that are not strictly necessary in relation to the relevant purposes.

Accuracy

There are obvious risks to data subjects if inaccurate data are processed. Therefore controllers are responsible for taking all reasonable steps to ensure that personal data are accurate.

Personal data must be accurate and, where necessary, kept up to date. Every reasonable step must be taken to ensure that personal data that are inaccurate are either erased or rectified without delay.

The GDPR does not materially change the accuracy principle. The GDPR specifies that the erasure or rectification of inaccurate personal data must be implemented without delay, but that requirement is implicit in the wording of the Directive.

Data retention periods

The idea that personal data should not be retained for longer than necessary in relation to the purposes for which they were collected, or for which they are further processed, is key to ensuring fair processing.

Personal data must be kept in a form that permits identification of data subjects for no longer than is necessary for the purposes for which the personal data are processed. Personal data may be stored for longer periods insofar as the data will be processed solely for archiving purposes in the public interest, or scientific, historical, or statistical purposes in accordance with Art.89(1) and subject to the implementation of appropriate safeguards.

The principle should be read in light of the "right to be forgotten" under which data subjects have the right to erasure of personal data, in some cases sooner than the end of the maximum retention period.

Data security

Controllers are responsible for ensuring that personal data are kept secure; both against external threats (e.g., malicious hackers) and internal threats (e.g., poorly trained employees).

Personal data must be processed in a manner that ensures appropriate security of those data, including protection against unauthorised or unlawful processing and against accidental loss, destruction or damage, using appropriate technical or organisational measures.

The GDPR moves this obligation into the Data Protection Principles, reinforcing the idea that data security is a fundamental obligation of all controllers. However, the principle itself is essentially unchanged.

Accountability

The principle of accountability seeks to guarantee the enforcement of the Data Protection Principles. This principle goes hand-in-hand with the growing powers of DPAs.

The controller is responsible for, and must be able to demonstrate, compliance with the Data Protection Principles.

Under the GDPR, the controller is obliged to demonstrate that its processing activities are compliant with the Data Protection Principles. This obligation is expanded upon which sets out the obligations of controllers.

The changes introduced by the GDPR to the Data Protection Principles are not revolutionary. However, they do consolidate the importance of those principles in respect of data processing activities. In particular, the principles of transparency and minimisation of data, as well as the requirement of data integrity and confidentiality, are now clearly established as Data Protection Principles.

Article – 6 Lawfulness

Processing of personal data is lawful only if, and to the extent that, it is permitted under EU data protection law. If the controller does not have a lawful basis for a given data processing activity (and no exemption or derogation applies) then that activity is prima facie unlawful.

The nature of an organisation's business, and the sector in which it operates, makes no difference to that organisation's obligation to comply with EU data protection law. Hence, all types of organisations are affected.

Lawful basis

Under EU data protection law, there must be a lawful basis for all processing of personal data (unless an exemption or derogation applies).

"Personal may be processed only if, and to the extent that, at least one lawful basis applies."

The obligation on organisations to have a lawful basis in respect of each processing activity is essentially unchanged.

The "contractual performance" lawful basis permits the processing of personal data in two different scenarios:

- Situations in which processing is necessary for the performance of a contract to which the data subject is a party. This may include, for example, processing the address of the data subject so that goods purchased online can be delivered or processing credit card details in order to effect payment.
- …Situations that take place prior to entering into a contract such as pre-contractual relations (provided that steps are taken at the request of the data subject, rather than being initiated by the controller). For example, if an individual requests information from a retailer about a particular product, the processing of that individual's personal data is permitted for the purposes of responding to that enquiry.

Consent

Personal data may be processed on the basis that the data subject has consented to such processing.

"Processing is permitted if the data subject has consented to the processing."

"Consent" remains a lawful basis for processing personal data. However, under the GDPR, valid consent becomes significantly harder to obtain

Contractual necessity

Personal data may be processed on the basis that such processing is necessary in order to enter into or perform a contract with the data subject.

"Processing is permitted if it is necessary for the entry into, or performance of, a contract with the data subject or in order to take steps at his or her request prior to the entry into a contract."

"Contractual necessity" remains a lawful basis for processing personal data.

Compliance with legal obligations

Personal data may be processed on the basis that the controller has a legal obligation to perform such processing.

"Processing is permitted if it is necessary for compliance with a legal obligation."

"Compliance with legal obligations" remains a lawful basis for processing personal data.

Vital interests

Personal data may be processed on the basis that it is necessary to protect the "vital interests" of the data subject (this essentially applies in "life or-death" scenarios).

"Processing is permitted if it is necessary in order to protect the vital interests of the data subject or of another natural person."

Under the GDPR, the "vital interests" processing condition can extend to other individuals (e.g., children of the data subject). This is a helpful clarification

Public interest

Personal data may be processed on the basis that such processing is necessary for the performance of tasks carried out by a public authority or private organisation acting in the public interest.

"Processing is permitted if it is necessary for the performance of a task carried out in the public interest or in the exercise of official authority vested in the controller."

"Public interest" remains a lawful basis for processing personal data. Note also that processing carried out on this basis may be subject to objections from data subjects

Legitimate interests

Personal data may be processed on the basis that the controller has a legitimate interest in processing those data, provided that such legitimate interest is not overridden by the rights or freedoms of the affected data subjects.

"Processing is permitted if it is necessary for the purposes of legitimate interests pursued by the controller (or by a third party), except where the controller's interests are overridden by the interests, fundamental rights or freedoms of the affected data subjects which require protection, particularly where the data subject is a child."

This does not apply to processing carried out by public authorities in the performance of their duties.

"Legitimate interests" remains a lawful basis for processing personal data. Note also that processing carried out on this basis may be subject to objections from data subjects

Parental permission is required to process the personal data of children (and note that a child is anyone under the age of 16). In some contexts (especially online) proving that parental permission has been obtained may be difficult.

The "legitimate interests" lawful basis requires a balancing of the legitimate interests of the controller against the interests and fundamental rights of the data subject. To determine this balance, the controller should consider a number of factors, including:

- …the nature and source of the legitimate interest; ……
- whether the relevant processing activity is necessary for the exercise of a fundamental right, or is otherwise in the public interest;
- ……the impact on the data subject;
- ……the data subject's reasonable expectations about the processing of his or her personal data;
- ……the nature of the data and how those data are processed;
- ……additional safeguards that the controller can implement to limit any undue impact on the data subject (e.g., data minimisation, privacy-enhancing technologies, increased transparency, a right to opt-out, and data portability).

If, after weighing these factors, it is clear that the processing causes undue interference with the interests, rights, or freedoms of the affected data subjects, the organisation should not rely on the legitimate interests' legal basis.

Additional powers for Member States

Member States are permitted to introduce additional lawful bases for limited purposes connected with national law or the performance of tasks in the public interest.

"Member States may introduce additional lawful bases in relation to processing carried out for the purposes of complying with legal

obligations (see Art.6(1)(c) above) or performing tasks in the public interest (see Art.6(1)(e) above)."

This provision is largely intended to allow Member States to preserve certain lawful bases that exist under the national laws of the relevant Member States.

Data relating to criminal offences and civil law enforcement

Personal data relating to criminal offences are subject to additional restrictions (and are commonly treated as being analogous to Sensitive Personal Data) because of the potentially significant impact that the processing of such data can have upon the data subject .

It should be noted that the national criminal laws of Member States are outside the EU's legislative competence, and are not governed by the GDPR.

Personal data relating to criminal convictions and offences or related security measures may only be processed:

- *under the control of an official authority; or*
- *when permitted under EU or Member State law.*

"Any comprehensive register of criminal convictions may be kept only under the control of official authority.

Member States may impose restrictions on the processing of personal data for the purposes of enforcing civil law claims."

The restrictions concerning the processing of personal data relating to criminal offences or convictions, and civil law enforcement matters, do not materially change.

Processing Sensitive Personal Data

"The processing of Sensitive Personal Data is only permitted under certain conditions:

- Explicit consent - *The data subject has given explicit consent.*
- Employment law - *The processing is necessary in the context of employment law, or laws relating to social security and social protection.*
- Vital interests - *The processing is necessary to protect vital interests of the data subject (or another person) here the data subject is incapable of giving consent.*
- Charity or not-for-profit bodies - *The processing s carried out in the course of the legitimate activities of a charity or not-for-profit body, with respect to its own members, former members, or persons with whom it has regular contact in connection with its purposes.*
- Data manifestly made public by the data subject - *The processing relates to personal data which have been manifestly made public by the data subject.*
- Legal claims - *The processing is necessary for the establishment, exercise or defence of legal claims, or for courts acting in their judicial capacity.*
- Reasons of substantial public interest - *The processing is necessary for reasons of substantial public interest, and occurs on the basis of a law that is, inter alia, proportionate to the aim pursued and protects the rights of data subjects.*
- Public health - *The processing is necessary for reasons of public interest in the area of public health (e.g., ensuring the safety of medicinal products).*
- Historical, statistical or scientific purposes - *The processing is necessary for archiving purposes in the public interest, for historical, scientific, research or statistical purposes, subject to appropriate safeguards.*
- Exemptions under national law - *Member States may maintain or introduce further conditions, including*

> *limitations with regard to genetic data, biometric data or health data.*
> - *Medical diagnosis and treatment- The processing is required for the purpose of medical treatment undertaken by health professionals, including assessing the working capacity of employees and the management of health or social care systems and services."*

Article 7: Conditions for consent

Processing of personal data is lawful only if it is permitted under EU data protection law. Consequently, every data processing activity must require a lawful basis. As an example consent provides a lawful basis for processing personal data so long as it meets the regulation standards. Without a lawful basis, the processing of personal data is unlawful, and runs the risk of incurring substantial fines

The need for consent

All processing of personal data requires a lawful basis and consent provides one such lawful basis.

"In order for the processing of personal data to be lawful, the controller requires either the consent of the data subject or another lawful basis."

The GDPR makes no material change to the principle that consent may provide a lawful basis for data processing activities. However, as set out below, the GDPR makes it significantly more difficult for organisations to obtain valid consent.

Nature of valid consent

The consent of the data subject provides a lawful basis for the processing of that data subject's personal data. However, such consent must meet certain requirements in order to be deemed sufficient for the purposes of EU data protection law.

"Consent" means any freely given, specific, informed and unambiguous indication of the data subject's agreement to the processing of his or her personal data. Consent must be given by a statement or a clear affirmative action.

The Directive only states that the data subject must "signify" consent. The GDPR makes it clear that consent requires a clear affirmative action by the data subject. This may make it harder for some organisations to obtain valid consent.

Consent must be "freely given"

Consent must reflect the data subject's genuine and free choice. If there is any element of compulsion, or undue pressure put upon the data subject, consent will not be valid.

"Consent will not be valid if the data subject has no genuine and free choice, or is unable to refuse or withdraw consent without detriment.

Where there is a "clear imbalance" between the controller and the data subject (e.g., between an employer and an employee), consent is presumed not to have been freely given.

When assessing whether consent is freely given, utmost account must be taken of whether the performance of a contract is made conditional on the data subject consenting to processing activities that are not necessary for the performance of that contract."

The Directive provides almost no guidance on the meaning of the phrase "freely given". The GDPR makes it significantly harder for organisations to demonstrate that the data subject's consent has been freely given. For example some instances where it may be contentious are between an employer and employee, or a Public \ Government Office and a Citizen. Therefore some useful pointers:

- organisations must ensure that data subjects have a genuine choice;
- organisations should consider whether to rely on consent as a lawful basis for processing the personal data of their own employees; and
- wherever possible, organisations should avoid making the performance of a contract conditional upon the data subject's consent to the processing of personal data.

Consent must be "specific"

Blanket consent that does not specify the exact purpose of the processing is not valid consent.

"Consent" must be specific. The GDPR does not explain this term further.

It is important to understand that consent must be intelligible. Therefore it is up to the controller to clearly and precisely explain the scope and the consequences of the data processing. In addition consent cannot apply to an open-ended set of processing activities—it must be limited to a specific purpose.

Consent must be "informed"

In order for consent to be valid, data subjects must be provided with sufficient information to enable them to understand what they are consenting to.

"Consent must be "informed". In order for consent to be informed:

- *the nature of the processing should be explained in an intelligible and easily accessible form, using clear and plain language which does not contain unfair terms; and*
- *the data subject should be aware at least of the identity of the controller and the purposes for which the personal data will be processed."*

The GDPR requires organisations to take significant efforts to ensure that data subjects are properly informed of the purposes for which their personal data will be used. Consent must be 'informed' to ensure that data subjects understand the risks associated with the processing of their personal data. The information to be provided to data subjects should include:

- the identity of the controller (and, where appropriate, its representative);
- the purposes for which the data will be processed;
- any further information that is necessary to enable the data subject to understand the processing to which they are being asked to consent (e.g., the third parties with whom the data may be shared;
- the existence of the right of access to, and the right to rectify, personal data;
- the existence of the right to object to processing and the right to be forgotten; and
- the existence of the right to withdraw consent.

If this information is not provided in line with these requirements, any "consent" obtained may not be valid.

Method of obtaining consent

EU data protection law does not specify the method by which consent should be obtained. Therefore, an organisation may use any appropriate mechanism to obtain consent.

However, there are requirements as to how consent may be provided. Hence, consent may be sought using any appropriate method but consent must only be provided in the form of a clear, affirmative action of the data subject. A notable point is that obtaining consent should be from the data subject – first hand as generally consent cannot be obtained from a third party although there are some exceptions such as in the case of parents providing consent in relation to their children.

Another point to be aware of is that the consent itself must be something that the data subject has said or done to indicate that they agree to the processing of their personal data. This affirmative action to signal an agreement can take any appropriate form such as a signature, a tick-box, or even a verbal consent but it must be an affirmative action. It is no longer acceptable to consider passive acquiescence or failure to opt-out or mere silence/non-action – GDPR seems to take particular umbrage against the use of pre-ticked boxes - as acceptance as they do not constitute valid consent under the GDPR.

Consent must take the form of an affirmative action or statement.

"Consent can be provided by any appropriate method enabling a freely given, specific and informed indication of the data subject's wishes. For example, depending on the circumstances, valid consent could be provided verbally, in writing, by ticking a box on a web page, by choosing technical settings in an app, or by any other statement or conduct which clearly indicates in this context the data subject's acceptance of the proposed processing of their personal data."

The GDPR recognises that any appropriate method of collecting consent can be used but organisations should give careful thought to ensuring that their consent mechanisms are appropriate to the nature of the consent being sought.

Silence is not consent

Acquiescence is not the same thing as consent. The fact that a data subject says nothing when given the opportunity to object, or fails to opt-out or unsubscribe, will not amount to valid consent.

"Silence, pre-ticked boxes, inactivity, failure to opt-out, or passive acquiescence does not constitute valid consent."

The current Directive does not specifically state that silence and inactivity are not consent so the GDPR makes the point extremely clear. Organisations should ensure that they do not rely on silence or inactivity as consent.

Consent must be distinguishable from other matters

What this means is that a data subject's consent to the processing of his or her personal data should not be conditional or tied to other matters.

"If consent is given in the context of a written declaration which also concerns other matters, the request for consent must be presented in a manner which is clearly distinguishable from the other matters, in an intelligible and easily accessible form, using clear and plain language. If the data subject is asked to consent to something that is inconsistent with the requirements of the GDPR, that consent will not be binding."

The GDPR clear up any potential ambiguity that may have existed with the current directive and it makes the point extremely clear, emphasising its importance by stating that consent language that is inconsistent with the requirements of the GDPR is non-binding. Organisations should ensure that consent to the processing of personal data is always clearly distinguished from other matters for example that consent is not wrapped up as part of a wider set of terms and conditions.

The controller must be able to demonstrate consent

A data subject may challenge that they actually consented to the processing of his or her personal data consequently a controller must be able to demonstrate how and when they obtained the consent.

"Where any processing activity is performed on the basis of consent, the controller must be able to demonstrate that it has obtained valid consent from the affected data subjects."

Currently the Directive does not specifically require controllers to retain evidence of consent. The GDPR places the burden of proof on the controller.

Right of data subjects to withdraw consent

Data subjects must be able to withdraw their consent. However, the right of data subjects to withdraw consent is not retrospective (i.e., data subjects cannot withdraw consent to processing that has already happened).

"Data subjects have the right to withdraw their consent at any time. The withdrawal of consent does not affect the lawfulness of processing based on consent before its withdrawal. Prior to giving consent, the data subject must be informed of the right to withdraw consent. It must be as easy to withdraw consent as to give it."

The Directive does not state that there is a right to withdraw consent. However this right has generally been enforced by DPAs. The GDPR formalises this right, and obliges organisations to make it easy for individuals to withdraw consent. This obligation may require businesses to review systems and procedures as consent may be withdrawn at any time.

Consent can provide a lawful data transfer mechanism

If the data subject has consented to the transfer of his or her personal data to a jurisdiction outside the EEA, that consent provides a lawful data transfer mechanism

"In the absence of other safeguards, transfers may take place if the data subject has explicitly consented to the transfer, having previously been informed of its possible risks. This does not apply to public authorities in the exercise of their powers."

The GDPR makes no material change to the principle that consent may provide a lawful data transfer mechanism, but it explicitly names it as a legal basis for Cross-Border Data Transfers.

Impact of the GDPR on existing consent

As the GDPR set the bar higher for consent any existing consents that are valid under the current Directive, but do not satisfy the requirements of the GDPR, will have to be re-obtained.

"Where an organisation has already collected consent from data subjects (prior to the GDPR Effective Date) it is not necessary to collect that consent a second time in consequence of the GDPR, provided that the initial consent was compliant with the requirements of the GDPR."

In many cases, historic consents – if they were ever obtained - will not be compliant with the requirements of the GDPR, and in such cases it will be necessary to collect fresh consents. This is especially true old legacy CRM systems and for some organisations retrospectively reviewing and obtaining lawful consent will be an onerous task.

Article 8: Conditions applicable to child's consent in relation to information society services

"Where point (a) of Article 6(1) applies, in relation to the offer of information society services directly to a child, the processing of the personal data of a child shall be lawful where the child is at least 16 years old. Where the child is below the age of 16 years, such processing shall be lawful only if and to the extent that consent is given or authorised by the holder of parental responsibility over the child."

There is the option for Member States to lower the limit from 16 years to 13 years to bring them in line with US regulations as having a disparity could have caused major issues for international organisations. The UK for example was to exercise this right and lower the age restriction to 13. Regardless of the age limit set:

"The controller shall make reasonable efforts to verify in such cases that consent is given or authorised by the holder of parental responsibility over the child, taking into consideration available technology."

Article 9: Processing of special categories of personal data

Permissions to process special category personal data

Processing of personal data revealing racial or ethnic origin, political opinions, religious or philosophical beliefs, or trade union membership, and the processing of genetic data, biometric data for the purpose of uniquely identifying a natural person, data concerning health or data concerning a natural person's sex life or sexual orientation shall be prohibited.

However the conditions prohibiting the processing of special category personal data will not apply under certain circumstances:

Act 9

a) the data subject has given explicit consent to the processing of those personal data for one or more specified purposes,

(b) processing is necessary for the purposes of carrying out the obligations and exercising specific rights of the controller or of the data subject in the field of employment and social security and social protection law in so far as it is authorised by Union or Member State law

(c) processing is necessary to protect the vital interests of the data subject or of another natural person where the data subject is physically or legally incapable of giving consent;

(d) processing is carried out in the course of its legitimate activities with appropriate safeguards by a foundation, association or any other not-for-profit body with a political, philosophical, religious or trade union aim

(e) processing relates to personal data which are manifestly made public by the data subject;

(f) processing is necessary for the establishment, exercise or defence of legal claims or whenever courts are acting in their judicial capacity;

(g) processing is necessary for reasons of substantial public interest, on the basis of Union or Member State law

(h) processing is necessary for the purposes of preventive or occupational medicine,

(i) processing is necessary for reasons of public interest in the area of public health, such as protecting against serious cross-border threats to health or ensuring high standards of quality and safety of health care and of medicinal products or medical devices,

(j) processing is necessary for archiving purposes in the public interest, scientific or historical research

Member States may maintain or introduce further conditions, including limitations, with regard to the processing of genetic data, biometric data or data concerning health.-

Article 10: Processing of data relating to criminal convictions and offences

Processing Criminal Records

Act 10

Processing of personal data relating to criminal convictions and offences or related security measures based on Article 6(1) shall be carried out only under the control of official authority or when the processing is authorised by Union or Member State law providing for appropriate safeguards for the rights and freedoms of data subjects.

Article 11: Processing which does not require identification

Processing not allowing identification

There will be cases where s Controller collects personal data which cannot be identified or no longer requires identifying a data subject then:

Act 11

If the purposes for which a controller processes personal data do not or do no longer require the identification of a data subject by the controller, the controller shall not be obliged to maintain, acquire or process additional information in order to identify the data subject for the sole purpose of complying with this Regulation.

Chapter 3: Rights of the Data Subject

Section 1: Transparency and Modalities
Article 12: Transparent information, communication and modalities for the exercise of the rights of the data subject

Section 2: Information and Access to Data
Article 13: Information to be provided where personal data are collected from the data subject
Article 14: Information to be provided where personal data have not been obtained from the data subject
Article 15: Right of access by the data subject

Section 3: Rectification and Erasure
Article 16: Right to rectification
Article 17: Right to erasure ('right to be forgotten')
Article 18: Right to restriction of processing
Article 18: Right to data portability
Article 19: Notification obligation regarding rectification or erasure of personal data or restriction of processing

Article 20: Right to data portability

Section 4: Right to object and automated individual decision making
Article 21: Right to object
Article 22: Automated individual decision-making, including profiling

Section 5: Restrictions
Article 23: Restrictions

Article 12: Transparent information, communication and modalities for the exercise of the rights of the data subject

Transparent communication

To ensure the fair processed of personal data, the EU data protection law obliges controllers to communicate transparently with data subjects regarding the processing of their personal data.

Art.5(1)(a), 12-14

In order to ensure that personal data are processed fairly and lawfully, controllers must provide certain minimum information to data subjects, regarding the collection and further processing of their personal data. Such information must be provided in a concise, transparent, intelligible and easily accessible form, using clear and plain language. Any information provided to children should be in such a clear and plain language that the child can easily understand

Both the current Directive and the GDPR require that controllers provide information that is transparent, concise, legible, etc. In addition the information provided by the controller to the data subject should not consist of privacy policies that are excessively verbose, lengthy or difficult to understand.

Rights of data subjects

Controllers are obliged to give effect to the rights of data subjects under EU data protection law.

Art.12(2)

Controllers have a legal obligation to give effect to the rights of data subjects.

In effect, controllers are required to give effect to the rights of data subjects under the Directive. The GDPR merely formalises the de facto position under the Directive.

Identifying data subjects

To address security vulnerability where a third parties might attempt to exercise a data subject's rights without proper authorisation to do so Controllers are therefore permitted to challenge data subjects to provide proof of their identity before giving effect to their rights.

Art.12(2), (6)

The controller must not refuse to give effect to the rights of a data subject unless the controller cannot identify the data subject. The controller must use all reasonable efforts to verify the identity of data subjects. Where the controller has reasonable doubts as to the identity of the data subject, the controller may request the provision of additional information necessary to confirm the identity of the data subject, but is not required to do so

The GDPR explicitly enables controllers to require data subjects to provide proof of identity before giving effect to their rights. This helps to limit the risk that third parties gain unlawful access to personal data. Notably the controller however is under no such obligation to do so.

Exemption where the controller cannot identify the data subject

If the controller cannot reasonably identify the data subject, the controller is exempt from the obligation for the application of certain rights of that data subject.

Art.11, 12(2)

To the extent that the controller can demonstrate that it is not in a position to identify the data subject, the controller is exempt from the application of the rights of data subjects in Art.15-22. The controller is also not obliged to obtain further personal data in order to link data in its possession to a data subject.

Under the GDPR the controller is exempt from its obligation to comply with certain rights of data subjects if it cannot identify which data in its possession relate to the relevant data subject.

Time limits for complying with the rights of data subjects

Controllers are obliged to give effect to the rights of data subjects within specified time periods, in order to avoid the frustration of those rights through excessive delays.

Art.12(3)-(4)

A controller must, within one month of receiving a request made under those rights, provide any requested information in relation to any of the rights of data subjects. If the controller fails to meet this deadline, the data subject may complain to the relevant DPA and may seek a judicial remedy. Where a controller receives large numbers of requests, or especially complex requests, the time limit may be extended by a maximum of two further months.

The introduction of specified time limits under the GDPR results in more onerous compliance obligations for controllers.

Article 13: Information to be provided where personal data are collected from the data subject

Right to basic information

A core principle of EU data protection law is that data subjects should be entitled to a minimum set of information concerning the purposes for which their personal data will be processed.

Art.13-14

Data subjects have the right to be provided with information on the identity of the controller, the reasons for processing their personal data and other relevant information necessary to ensure the fair and transparent processing of personal data.

The GDPR largely preserves the position as it stands under the Directive—the requirement to ensure transparency is implied in the Directive. Organisations remain obliged to provide basic information to individuals.

Article 14: Information to be provided where personal data have not been obtained from the data subject

Data obtained indirectly i.e. not from the data subject

Where personal data have not been obtained from the data subject, the controller shall provide the data subject with the following information:

Act 14

(a) the identity and the contact details of the controller and, where applicable, of the controller's representative;

(b) the contact details of the data protection officer, where applicable;

(c) the purposes of the processing for which the personal data are intended as well as the legal basis for the processing;

(d) the categories of personal data concerned;

(e) the recipients or categories of recipients of the personal data, if any;

(f) where applicable, that the controller intends to transfer personal data to a recipient in a third country or international organisation and the existence or absence of an adequacy decision by the Commission, or in the case of transfers referred to in Article 46 or 47, or the second subparagraph of Article 49(1), reference to the appropriate or suitable safeguards and the means to obtain a copy of them or where they have been made available.

This is in addition to the standard requirement of information that a controller must give a data subject such as data retention time, purpose, third party access etc.

Article 15: Right of access by the data subject

Right of access

In order to allow data subjects to enforce their data protection rights, EU data protection law obliges controllers to provide data subjects with access to their personal data.

Art.15

Data subjects have the right to obtain:

- *confirmation of whether, and where, the controller is processing their personal data;*
- *information about the purposes of the processing;*
- *information about the categories of data being processed;*
- *information about the categories of recipients with whom the data may be shared;*

- *information about the period for which the data will be stored (or the criteria used to determine that period);*
- *information about the existence of the rights to erasure, to rectification, to restriction of processing and to object to processing;*
- *information about the existence of the right to complain to the DPA;*
- *where the data were not collected from the data subject, information as to the source of the data; and*
- *information about the existence of, and an explanation of the logic involved in, any automated processing that has a significant effect on data subjects.*

Additionally, data subjects may request a copy of the personal data being processed.

The GDPR expands the mandatory categories of information which must be supplied in connection with a data subject access request (SAR). Such requests can be time consuming, excessive in nature and may be unfounded therefore they are likely to place an even greater administrative burden on organisations.

Fees in respect of access requests

In order to dissuade data subjects from making vexatious requests, data controllers are permitted to charge a small fee for each such request.

Art.12(5), 15(3), (4)

The controller must give effect to the rights of access, rectification, erasure and the right to object, free of charge. The controller may charge a reasonable fee for "repetitive requests", "manifestly unfounded or excessive requests" or "further copies".

The Directive permits controllers to charge a small fee for certain functions (e.g., responding to the right of access). This acts as a buffer against spurious or fishing-exercise type requests. The GDPR does not permit such charges in most cases. There is, therefore, an elevated risk that individuals will attempt to exercise these rights merely because they can, or as a cheap but effective means of protest against an organisation. As a result the GDPR does allow the controller to charge for *"repetitive requests", "manifestly unfounded or excessive requests" or "further copies* but the onus is firmly on them to prove the requests are excessive or unfounded.

Article 16: Right to rectification

Right of rectification

Data subjects are entitled to require a controller to rectify any errors in their personal data.

Art.5(1)(d), 16

Controllers must ensure that inaccurate or incomplete data are erased or rectified. Data subjects have the right to rectification of inaccurate personal data.

The position under the GDPR is largely unchanged, and organisations are likely to face the same requirements under the GDPR as under the Directive, in relation to the right of rectification.

Article 17: Right to erasure ('right to be forgotten')

Right to erasure (the "right to be forgotten")

Data subjects are entitled to require a controller to delete their personal data if the continued processing of those data is not justified.

Art.17

Data subjects have the right to erasure of personal data (the "right to be forgotten") if:

- *the data are no longer needed for their original purpose (and no new lawful purpose exists);*
- *the lawful basis for the processing is the data subject's consent, the data subject withdraws that consent, and no other lawful ground exists;*
- *the data subject exercises the right to object, and the controller has no overriding grounds for continuing the processing;*
- *the data have been processed unlawfully; or*
- *erasure is necessary for compliance with EU law or the national law of the relevant Member State.*

The "right to be forgotten" states that data subjects have the right to require an organisation that holds their personal data to delete those data where the retention of those data is not compliant with the requirements of the GDPR. Provided that an organisation has a lawful basis for processing personal data other than based on consent, it will not be significantly affected by the right to be forgotten. For example news and media publishing organizations will not significantly be affected.

Article 18: Right to restriction of processing

The right to restrict processing

In some circumstances, data subjects may not be entitled to require the controller to erase their personal data, but may be entitled to limit the purposes for which the controller can process those data.

Art.18

Data subjects have the right to restrict the processing of personal data (meaning that the data may only be held by the controller, and may only be used for limited purposes) if:

- *the accuracy of the data is contested (and only for as long as it takes to verify that accuracy);*

- *the processing is unlawful and the data subject requests restriction (as opposed to exercising the right to erasure);*
- *the controller no longer needs the data for their original purpose, but the data are still required by the controller to establish, exercise or defend legal rights; or*
- *if verification of overriding grounds is pending, in the context of an erasure request.*

Under the GDPR, organisations face a much broader range of circumstances in which data subjects can require that the processing of their personal data is restricted.

Article 19: Notification obligation regarding rectification or erasure of personal data or restriction of processing

Notifying third parties regarding rectification, erasure or restriction

In order to protect the rights of data subjects all parties who are processing the relevant data should be aware that the data subject has exercised those rights. Therefore, the onus is on the controllers to notify any third parties with whom they have shared the relevant data that the data subject has exercised those rights.

Art.17(2), 19

Where a controller has disclosed personal data to any third parties, and the data subject has subsequently exercised any of the rights of rectification, erasure or blocking, the controller must notify those third parties of the data subject's exercising of those rights. The controller is exempt from this obligation if it is impossible or would require disproportionate effort. The data subject is also entitled to request information about the identities of those third parties. Where the controller has made the data public, and the data subject exercises these rights, the controller must take reasonable steps (taking costs into account) to inform third parties that the data subject has exercised those rights

For organisations that disclose personal data to a large number of third parties, this may be particularly burdensome article as in addition to giving effect to the new rights that the GDPR grants to data subjects, organisations are also required to notifying affected third parties about the exercise of those rights and this may entail new systems and procedures.

Article 20: Right to data portability

Right of data portability

Data subjects have the right to transfer their personal data between controllers for example to move accounts from one online service provider platform to another such as an email account).

Art.20

Data subjects have a right to receive a copy of their personal data in a commonly used machine-readable format, and transfer their personal data from one controller to another or have the data transmitted directly between controllers.

For some organisations, this new right to transfer personal data between controllers creates a significant additional burden, requiring substantial investment in new systems and processes.

However, other organisations, may find the right to transfer personal data between controllers creates a significant opportunity to attract customers from competitors under the GDPR, as the competitor must allow the account information to be transferred.

Section 4: Right to object and automated individual decision making

Article 21: Right to object

Many organisations currently rely on "legitimate interests" as a lawful basis for the processing of personal data. As set out in this Chapter, the GDPR permits data subjects to object to the processing of their personal data on this basis. However, the GDPR reverses the burden of proof for rather than the data subject having to demonstrate justified grounds for objecting, the controller must demonstrate "compelling legitimate grounds for the processing which override the interests, rights and freedoms of the data subject".

As a result, many businesses may find that they are no longer able to rely on legitimate interests as a lawful basis for the processing of personal data in the course of their ordinary business activities.

Right to object to processing

A controller must have a lawful basis for processing personal data. However, where that lawful basis is either "public interest" or "legitimate interests", those lawful bases are not absolute hence data subjects may have a right to object to such processing.

Art.21

Data subjects have the right to object, on grounds relating to their particular situation, to the processing of personal data, where the basis for that processing is either:

- *public interest; or*
- *legitimate interests of the controller.*

The controller must cease such processing unless the controller:

- *demonstrates compelling legitimate grounds for the processing which override the interests, rights and freedoms of the data subject; or*
- *requires the data in order to establish, exercise or defend legal rights*

Whereas the current Directive permits an organisation to continue processing the relevant data unless the data subject can show that the objection is justified. The GDPR requires the organisation to demonstrate that it either has compelling grounds for continuing the processing, or that the processing is necessary in connection with its legal rights. If it cannot demonstrate that the relevant processing activity is lawful, it must cease that processing activity. This will be a significant issue for organisations that currently rely on their own legitimate interests as a lawful basis for processing personal data.

Right to object to processing for the purposes of direct marketing

Data subjects have the right to object to the processing of their personal data for the purposes of direct marketing.

Art.21(2)-(3)

Data subjects have the right to object to the processing of personal data for the purpose of direct marketing, including profiling.

The GDPR maintains the position as it stands under the Directive. It should be noted that data subjects also have rights in respect of direct marketing under the current ePrivacy Directive.

Right to object to processing for scientific, historical or statistical purposes

Personal data may be processed for scientific, historical or statistical purposes in the public interest, but individuals have a right to object to such processing.

Art.21(6), 83(1)

Where personal data are processed for scientific and historical research purposes or statistical purposes, the data subject has the right to object, unless the processing is necessary for the performance of a task carried out for reasons of public interest.

The GDPR provides individuals a more specific right to object than the rights available under the Directive.

Obligation to inform data subjects of the right to object

Controllers are obliged to inform data subjects of their rights to object to processing.

Art.13(2)(b), 14(2)(c), 15(1)(e), 21(4)

The right to object to processing of personal data noted above must be communicated to the data subject no later than the time of the first communication with the data subject.

This information should be provided clearly and separately from any other information provided to the data subject.

Controllers are obliged to provide additional information to data subjects. For many organisations, this will require revisions to standard data protection policies and privacy notices.

Article 22: Automated individual decision-making, including profiling

Right to not be evaluated on the basis of automated processing

Data subjects have the right not to be evaluated in any material sense solely on the basis of automated processing of their personal data.

Rec.71, 75; Art.22

Data subjects have the right not to be subject to a decision based solely on automated processing which significantly affect them (including profiling). Such processing is permitted where:

- *it is necessary for entering into or performing a contract with the data subject provided that appropriate safeguards are in place;*
- *it is authorised by law; or*
- *the data subject has explicitly consented and appropriate safeguards are in place.*

The GDPR clarifies that the consent of the data subject is a valid basis for evaluation on the basis of automated profiling.

Section 5: Restrictions

Article 23: Restrictions

Chapter 4: Controller and Processor

Section 1: General Obligations
Article 24: Responsibility of the controller
Article 25: Data protection by design and by default
Article 26: Joint controllers
Article 27: Representatives of controllers not established in the Union
Article 28: Processor
Article 29: Processing under the authority of the controller or processor
Article 30: Records of processing activities
Article 31: Cooperation with the supervisory authority

Section 2: Security of personal data

Article 32: Security of processing
Article 33: Notification of a personal data breach to the supervisory authority
Article 34: Communication of a personal data breach to the data subject

Section 3: Data protection impact assessment and prior consultation
Article 35: Data protection impact assessment
Article 36: Prior Consultation

Section 4: Data protection officer
Article 37: Designation of the data protection officer
Article 38: Position of the data protection officer
Article 39: Tasks of the data protection officer

Section 5: Codes of conduct and certification
Article 40: Codes of Conduct
Article 41: Monitoring of approved codes of conduct
Article 42: Certification
Article 43: Certification Bodies

Article 24: Responsibility of the controller

Definition of "controller"

In general terms, the "controller" is the entity that determines the purposes for which and the means by which personal data are processed i.e. they are the instigators and architect of the 'Why' and the 'How' of data processing.

In summary, a "controller" is an entity that, alone or jointly with others, determines how and why personal data are processed.

Accountability

The principle of accountability seeks to guarantee the enforcement of the Data Protection Principles. This principle goes hand-in-hand with the growing powers of DPAs.

Art.5(2)

The controller is responsible for, and must be able to demonstrate, compliance with the Data Protection Principles.

Responsibility of controllers

In general, controllers bear primary responsibility for ensuring that processing activities are compliant with EU data protection law.

Art.24

The controller is responsible for implementing appropriate technical and organisational measures to ensure and to demonstrate that its processing activities are compliant with the requirements of the GDPR. These measures may include implementing an appropriate privacy policy. Adherence to approved Codes of Conduct (see Chapter 12) may provide evidence of compliance.

A controller is responsible for ensuring that its processing activities are lawful. The GDPR provides the detail on how organisations can demonstrate that their processing activities are lawful.

Article 25: Data protection by design and by default

Organisations must ensure that for each current or proposed data processing activity, they must take proactive measures to "design in" data protection compliance. Hence, when introducing new or developing existing product or service that involves additional processing of personal data, organisations must ensure that the relevant product or service is designed with data protection compliance in mind.

In addition, organisations must process personal data in accordance with the rights afforded to individuals under the GDPR by default. This may mean that many businesses will have to re-think their data processing activities.

Data protection by design and by default

This principle means that compliance with EU data protection law should not be an after-thought, but as a key factor in the planning and implementation of any new product or service that affects personal data.

Art.25

Controllers must ensure that, both in the planning phase of processing activities and the implementation phase of any new product or service, Data Protection Principles, and appropriate safeguards, are addressed and implemented. For example, the controller must implement measures that provide for the security of any data processed, and give effect to the rights of data subjects

The GDPR imposes on organisations a requirement to ensure that data protection compliance is designed into their data processing activities. Similarly, organisations are required, by default, to process only the minimum amount of personal data necessary.

Article 26: Joint controllers

Joint controllers

In relation to any processing activity, it is possible for more than one entity to be the controller for example in a joint venture between equal partners.

Art.4(7), 26

Where two or more controllers jointly determine the purposes and means of the processing of personal data, they are joint controllers.

Joint controllers must, by means of an "arrangement" between them, apportion data protection compliance responsibilities between themselves).

A summary of the arrangement must be made available for the data subject. The arrangement may designate a contact point for data subjects.

In some scenarios where processing takes place internal to organisations the relationship between controllers and processors may not be clear and the organisation may not realise that there is joint controllership. The GDPR places an obligation on such organisations to keep watch for potential instances of joint controllership.

Liability of joint controllers

Where liability arises in a joint controllership scenario, EU data protection law's primary focus is on ensuring that the data subject is protected.

Art.26(3), 82(3)-(5)

Data subjects are entitled to enforce their rights against any of the joint controllers. Each joint controller is liable for the entirety of the damage, although national law may apportion liability between them. A controller may be exempted from liability if it proves that it is not in any way responsible for the damage. If one joint controller has paid full compensation, it may then bring proceedings against the other joint controllers to recover their portions of the damages.

The GDPR makes joint controllers fully liable. Once "full compensation" has been paid to the affected data subject(s), joint controllers may recover damages from one another. This means that some joint controllers may find themselves facing much higher liability for claims made under the GDPR.

Under the existing Directive, joint controllers are generally only liable for the harm for which they are responsible. In practice this has meant that data subjects may not be able to obtain full compensation for any harm arising from the joint processing. However, the GDPR makes each of the joint controllers fully liable to the data subject. The data subject is therefore entitled to bring a claim against either of the joint controllers. As the data subject's protection is paramount it is only once "full compensation" has been paid, that the joint controller(s) who paid that compensation may then seek to recover damages from any other joint controllers involved in the joint processing. It is likely that, under the GDPR, joint controllers will increasingly seek contractual indemnities from one another prior to commencing any joint processing.

Article 27: Representatives of controllers not established in the Union

Appointment of representatives

Where EU data protection law applies to a controller or a processor established outside the EU that controller or processor is obliged to appoint a representative based in the EU, as a point of contact for EU data subjects and DPAs.

Art.4(17), 27

A controller established outside the EU must appoint a representative in one of the Member States in which the controller offers goods or services or monitors EU residents, unless the processing is occasional, small-scale and does not involve Sensitive Personal Data. The appointment of the representative is without prejudice to legal actions which could be initiated against the controller. The representative must be mandated by the controller or processor to be addressed in addition to or instead of the controller or the processor by supervisory authorities and data subjects, on all issues related to data protection. A representative may be subject to enforcement actions by DPAs in the event of non-compliance by the controller.

Non-EU organisations that are occasional, small-scale operations not involving Sensitive Personal Data are not obliged to appoint a representative under the GDPR. Importantly, a representative may be liable for the controller's failure to comply with the GDPR so should not be entered into without strong contractual indemnities in place.

Article 28 - Appointment of processors

Processors

Organisations that act as controllers commonly appoint service providers to process personal data on their behalf. EU data protection law permits this practice, but imposes certain requirements on organisations that wish to do so.

Art.28(1)-(3)

A controller that wishes to appoint a processor must only use processors that guarantee compliance with the GDPR. The controller must appoint the processor in the form of a binding agreement in writing, which states that the processor must:

- *only act on the controller's documented instructions;*
- *impose confidentiality obligations on all personnel who process the relevant data;*
- *ensure the security of the personal data that it processes;*
- *abide by the rules regarding appointment of sub-processors;*
- *implement measures to assist the controller in complying with the rights of data subjects;*
- *assist the controller in obtaining approval from DPAs where required;*
- *at the controller's election, either return or destroy the personal data at the end of the relationship (except as required by EU or Member State law); and*

- *provide the controller with all information necessary to demonstrate compliance with the GDPR.*

The GDPR imposes significant new requirements that must be included in all data processing agreements. It is likely that processors located outside the EU will resist the imposition of these new obligations, potentially making it harder for controllers to lawfully appoint their desired processors, and resulting in more complex negotiation of outsourcing agreements.

Article 29: Processing under the authority of the controller or processor

Processing Authority

A processor must only processor data under the instructions and authority of their controller.

Art 29

The processor and any person acting under the authority of the controller or of the processor, who has access to personal data, shall not process those data except on instructions from the controller, unless required to do so by Union or Member State law.

This is not a significant change as a similar requirement exist under the Directive – "the processor shall act only on instructions from the controller".

Article 30: Records of processing activities

Records of processing activities

EU data protection law requires organisations to keep records of their data processing activities, and that the information in those records is provided to (or is available on request by) DPAs.

Art.30

There is no obligation to notify DPAs. Instead, each controller (and its representative, if any) must keep records of the controller's processing activities, including:

- *the contact details of the controller/representative/ DPO;*
- *the purposes of the processing;*
- *the categories of data subjects and personal data processed;*
- *the categories of recipients with whom the data may be shared;*
- *information regarding Cross-Border Data Transfers;*
- *the applicable data retention periods; and*
- *a description of the security measures implemented in respect of the processed data.*

Upon request, these records must be disclosed to DPAs.

The GDPR does away with the requirement to notify DPAs regarding an organisation's processing activities. Instead the obligation is now on organisations to identify and record their data processing activities and make them available to the DPA on request.

The GDPR provides an exemption for organisations employing fewer than 250 persons (unless the processing in question is of a high-risk nature).

Article 31: Cooperation with the supervisory authority

Cooperation with DPAs

DPAs are responsible for enforcing and regulating EU data protection law. Controllers are therefore required to cooperate with DPAs.

Art.31

Controllers (and their representatives, if any) are required to cooperate, on request, with DPAs in the performance of their tasks

The GDPR merely codifies the existing de facto (or, in some Member States, national legal) obligation of controllers to co-operate with DPAs.

Section 2: Security of personal data

Article 32: Security of processing

Data security

Security of the personal data that a Controller processes is a core concept in EU data protection law. Hence, the controller is obliged to abide by the principle of data security.

Art.32

The controller must implement appropriate technical and organisational security measures to protect personal data against accidental or unlawful destruction or loss, alteration, unauthorised disclosure or access. Depending on the nature of the processing, these measures may include:

- *encryption of the personal data;*
- *on-going reviews of security measures;*
- *redundancy and back-up facilities; and*
- *regular security testing.*

Adherence to an approved Code of Conduct may provide evidence that the controller has met these obligations.

The current Directive leaves a significant amount of discretion to the controller, in terms of the security mechanisms and processes they implement. With the GDPR is more prescriptive as the primary requirement is that the controller must ensure the security of the personal data that it processes.

Article 33: Notification of a personal data breach to the supervisory authority

Reporting data breaches to DPAs

Regulators can only take action in relation to data breaches if they are reported to them. Therefore, GDPR now requires controllers to report such breaches to DPAs in certain circumstances.

Art.33

In the event of a data breach, the controller must report the breach to the DPA without undue delay, and in any event within 72 hours of becoming aware of it. There is an exception where the data breach is unlikely to result in any harm to data subjects. The notification must include at least:

- *a description of the data breach, including the numbers of data subjects affected and the categories of data affected;*
- *the name and contact details of the DPO (or other relevant point of contact);*
- *the likely consequences of the data breach; and*
- *any measures taken by the controller to remedy or mitigate the breach.*

The controller must keep records of all data breaches, comprising the facts and effects of the breach and any remedial action taken.

Consequently the records of all data breaches no matter how small must be included in the controller's internal data processing records and these must be disclosed to DPAs on demand. For data breaches where there is significant risk of harm to data subjects the DPA must be informed within 72 hours. This may be one of the most onerous challenges introduced in the GDPR as the 72 hour deadline for reporting data breaches to DPAs will require organisations to identify, review and report data breaches under intense operational pressure. In addition, the notification obligations under the ePrivacy Directive continue to apply to telecommunications providers. Such organisations may therefore be required to notify a data breach twice (once under the GDPR and once under the ePrivacy Directive).

Article 34: Communication of a personal data breach to the data subject

Notifying data breaches to affected data subjects

EU data protection law requires controllers to notify breaches that affect data subjects in certain circumstances such as private data loss, compromise or disclosure.

Art.34

In the event of a data breach causing high risk to data subjects, the controller must notify the affected data subjects without undue delay. The notification must include at least:

- *the name and contact details of the DPO (or other relevant point of contact);*
- *the likely consequences of the data breach; and*
- *any measures taken by the controller to remedy or mitigate the breach.*

However, the controller may be exempt from this requirement if:

- *the risk of harm is remote because the affected data are protected (e.g., through strong encryption);*
- *the controller has taken measures to protect against the harm (e.g., suspending affected accounts); or*
- *the notification requires disproportionate effort (in which case the controller must issue a public notice of the breach).*

As data subjects can only take steps to protect themselves from adverse consequences of data breaches if they are aware of those breaches. The GDPR creates an obligation to notify data subjects of any such breach but this imposes a significant burden on organisations that process large volumes of personal data. This obligation also significantly increases the risk factor due to the threat of reputational harm which may arise as a consequence of a data breach. The exemptions provided under the GDPR largely reflect the position under existing national laws. Most importantly, if the risks associated with the breach – encryption, hashes, robust technical and organisational measures - have been effectively resolved then the organisation may be exempt from the notification requirements.

Section 3: Data protection impact assessment and prior consultation

Some organisations will be familiar with the concept of risk assessments and even Privacy Impact Assessments due to complying with the current Directive. However for those organizations that are not; a Privacy Impact Assessment is a step-by-step review of the relevant processing activity. Commonly referred to as a PIA the exercise is designed to examine each stage of a personal data processing activity, and help an organisation to ensure that it has identified and addressed all of the risks involved in that activity before it commences.

In the event that a DPA ever asks any questions about the relevant processing activity, the framework allows organisations to look back at a later date, and use the Privacy Impact Assessment to illustrate two important facts to the relevant DPA:

- All of the material risks were identified. An organisation can only comply with the requirements of data protection law if it has identified the material risks that arise in connection with its processing activities.
- Appropriate steps were taken to mitigate or accept those risks. In relation to each risk, the PIA framework provides a

record of the steps that were taken to resolve or mitigate any danger to the rights and freedoms of data subjects, and provides helpful guidance to organisations on achieving compliance.

Article 35: Data protection impact assessment

Impact Assessments

EU data protection law requires organisations to conduct an Impact Assessment to assess the potential risks arising out of any new personal data processing activity.

Art.35

Where a new processing activity is proposed (especially where new technologies will be used) resulting in a high degree of risk for data subjects, the controller must first conduct an Impact Assessment. A single Impact Assessment can cover multiple processing operations that present similar risks.

Conducting Privacy or Data Impact Assessments should not be a new requirement for controllers and most if not all DPAs would expect controllers to conduct Impact Assessments in relation to new, high-risk processing activities. Additionally, by conducting an Impact Assessment, controllers may identify and address risks that would otherwise not have been detected so it is considered an operational best practice.

Article 36: Prior Consultation

Prior Consultation

Whenever an organisation is planning to engage in a form of high risk processing that may potentially present risks to the rights and freedoms of data subjects, that organisation should consult the relevant DPA(s) for advice.

Art.35(4)-(6), 36

DPAs are responsible for creating a list of the types of processing that are subject to Impact Assessments. Those lists must be put through the Consistency Mechanism and then sent to the EDPB. Where a controller intends to engage in a processing activity on such a list, it must first consult with the relevant DPA.

The requirement to apply the Consistency Mechanism in respect of high risk processing activities should mean that businesses face more consistent enforcement measures from DPAs. However the additional burden of the obligation to conduct Impact Assessments imposes a new, and in some cases significant, compliance burden on controllers.

Section 4: Data protection officer

GDPR introduces a significant new governance burden for those organisations which are caught by the new requirement to appoint a DPO. Although this is already a requirement for most controllers in Germany under current data protection laws, it is an entirely new requirement (and cost) for many other EU member organisations. However the GDPR also provides explicit permission to appoint a single DPO for a corporate group and that can be seen as a welcome development for many organisations.

Article 37: Designation of the data protection officer

Appointment of a DPO

A DPO is a person who provides the primary contact point for data protection issues within an organisation.

Art.37

A controller or processor must appoint a DPO if local laws require it to do so, or if its data processing activities involve:

- *regular and systematic monitoring of data subjects on a large scale; or*
- *Processing Sensitive Personal Data on a large scale.*

A corporate group may collectively appoint a single DPO.

Organisations that are not required to appoint a DPO are free to do so voluntarily. If a DPO is appointed, the organisation must publish the details of the DPO, and communicate those details to the relevant DPA.

The obligation to appoint a DPO may impose a significant burden, especially for smaller organisations but many should consider whether they are mandated to appoint one.

Qualifications of a DPO

A DPO is responsible for data protection compliance. It therefore makes sense for organisations to ensure that their DPOs are suitably qualified for this role.

Art.37(5)-(6)

A DPO should have expert knowledge of data protection law and practice, and should be capable of performing the functions of a DPO (outlined below). A DPO can be an employee or an outside consultant.

It may well be challenging to find an existing employee who satisfies the prerequisite requirements of being a DPO. As a result this may mean that such organisations have to engage and designate as the DPO outside consultants.

Article 38: Position of the data protection officer

Role of a DPO

The role of the DPO is to ensure that the relevant organisation achieves data protection compliance.

Art.38(1)-(2), (4)-(5)

The DPO must deal with all data protection matters affecting the controller or processor properly and in a timely manner. The controller or processor must provide the DPO with the necessary resources and support. Data subjects may contact the DPO (e.g., to exercise their rights under the GDPR). The DPO must be bound by a confidentiality obligation in relation to his or her work.

The GDPR formalises requirements not expressly set out in the Directive.

Special protection for DPOs

The role of the DPO can be difficult as they can be seen to be working under a conflict of interest. The GDPR recognizes this and so makes it a protected position so in principle, an organisation should not be able to take disciplinary action against a DPO merely because the DPO enforces compliance. If an organisation could do so, it would leave the DPO unable to act in a truly independent manner.

Art.38(3)

The organisation cannot instruct the DPO in the performance of his or her duties, and cannot terminate the DPO's employment (or take any other disciplinary action) as a result of the performance of the DPO's duties.

Organisations should consider this issue very carefully, in conjunction with applicable employment laws in the relevant Member States. In practice, some organisations may conclude that it is better to appoint an outside consultant to the role of DPO, as opposed to an employee who will become very difficult to remove from that position.

Article 39: Tasks of the data protection officer

Tasks of a DPO

The DPO's role involves the performance of certain tasks, such as advising the relevant organisation of its data protection compliance obligations.

Art.38(6), 39

A DPO must fulfil at least the following tasks:

- *informing and advising the relevant controller or processor (and any employees who process personal data) about their obligations under the GDPR;*
- *monitor compliance with the GDPR by the controller or processor;*
- *advise on Impact Assessments and prior consultation with DPAs; and*
- *cooperate with DPAs and act as a point*

The DPO by fulfilling their tasks should, in theory, mean that the organisation is better able to achieve compliance with the GDPR.

Section 5: Codes of conduct and certification

The GDPR encourages the drawing up of Codes of Conduct by associations and other bodies representing categories of organisations, which should take into account the specific features of the various data processing sectors. Adherence to such Codes of Conduct may be used by controllers and processors to demonstrate compliance with the GDPR requirements. Furthermore, the GDPR encourages the implementation of seals and certifications. Organisations that adhere to either an approved Code of Conduct, or an approved seal or certification scheme, may be able to use such adherence as a means of differentiating themselves from their competitors. For example, an organisation that has achieved a seal that is specific to data protection in its industry is often permitted to display that seal publicly, as a means of demonstrating to individuals that it takes their data protection rights seriously. This, in turn, may persuade those individuals to do business with that organisation rather than with its competitors.

Article 40: Codes of Conduct

Purpose of Codes of Conduct

Codes of Conduct provide a means for certain industry sectors, or groups of organisations, to create context specific rules regarding the processing of personal data, in their respective industries, in compliance with EU data protection law.

Art.40 (2)

Associations and other industry bodies may prepare Codes of Conduct covering compliance with the GDPR, in respect of general or specific aspects of the GDPR.

The essential aim of the provisions relating to Codes of Conduct is the same in the Directive and the GDPR—in both cases, a Code of Conduct exists, and is adhered to by organisations, for the purpose of improving overall compliance with EU data protection law.

Encouragement of Codes of Conduct

Creating a Code of Conduct can help improve compliance. EU data protection law therefore obliges authorities to encourage the creation of Codes of Conduct so organizations should consider undertaking this sometimes tedious task.

Art.40(1), 57(1)(m), (p), (o)

Member States, DPAs and the EDPB are all obliged to encourage the drawing up of Codes of Conduct.

Adherence to Codes of Conduct by non-EEA controllers and processors

One of the core dangers of transferring data out of the EEA is that those data will be subject to lower standards of protection. By adhering to Codes of Conduct, non-EEA controllers and processors can address this risk, and provide a lawful basis for Cross-Border Data Transfers

Art.40(1)(j), (3), 46(2)(e)

Controllers and processors that are outside the EEA, and that are not subject to the GDPR, may adhere to Codes of Conduct in order to create a framework for providing adequate protection to personal data in third countries. The GDPR specifically allows adherence of non-EEA controllers and processors to an approved Code of Conduct to provide the basis for Cross-Border Data Transfers

One significant advantage establishing industry approved Codes of Conduct is the fact that non-EEA organisations can use adherence to approved Codes of Conduct as a basis for Cross-Border Data Transfers. This provides a new lawful option for organisations seeking to transfer personal data internationally. It may also make data transfer compliance simpler for organisations that exchange data with other organisations in the same industry.

Article 41: Monitoring of approved codes of conduct

Enforcement of Codes of Conduct

A Code of Conduct only serves a useful purpose to the extent that it is enforceable against entities that sign up to it. The question of who carries out such enforcement, and what powers they have for doing so, is therefore of critical importance to the operation of any Code of Conduct.

Art.40(4), 41

An independent body may be appointed by the relevant DPA to monitor and enforce a Code of Conduct if it is:

- *independent and has demonstrated its expertise;*
- *has established procedures for reviewing and assessing compliance with a Code of Conduct;*
- *has established procedures for dealing with complaints or infringements of the Code of Conduct; and*
- *can demonstrate that it has no conflicts of interest in this role.*

Such a body may be appointed to monitor and enforce compliance with a Code of Conduct. DPAs still retain their own separate enforcement powers.

A competent professional body that is familiar with the processing taking place within that industry may be better placed than a DPA to enforce a Code of Conduct. However, such bodies cannot act to the exclusion of DPAs, and a DPA can always intervene in any such enforcement proceedings.

Advantages of adherence to approved Codes of Conduct

Codes of Conduct clearly need to provide practical advantages for organisations, in order for the effort necessary to create such Codes of Conduct to be worthwhile.

Art.24(3), 28(5), 35(8), 46(2)(e), Art.83(2)(j)

Adherence to an approved Code of Conduct:

- *may provide guidance on specific compliance issues;*
- *may provide evidence of compliance with the GDPR;*
- *is a positive factor in an Impact Assessment;*
- *may provide the basis for Cross-Border Data Transfers); and*
- *may affect any fines imposed upon the adherent controller or processor.*

The increased advantages of adherence to an approved Code of Conduct create significant new reasons for organisations to consider creating and implementing Codes of Conduct.

Article 42: Certification

Purpose of seals and certifications

The primary purpose of seals and certifications is to provide organisations with a formally recognised confirmation of compliance with EU data protection law, typically with an associated visual symbol (e.g., a badge or emblem that can be displayed on published documents and websites, confirming that the organisation satisfies the requirements of the relevant seal or certification). Seals and certifications last for a maximum of three years, and may be renewed provided that the relevant conditions are still met. If the conditions are not met, the seal or certification may be withdrawn.

Art.42, 43

The GDPR provides for a voluntary system of accreditation, under which controllers or processors may adhere to the requirements of a seal or certification scheme, for the purpose of demonstrating compliance with the GDPR.

Although seals and certifications gain formal recognition under the GDPR, their essential purpose is unchanged: organisations that want a visual badge or emblem that demonstrates their compliance with all, or any aspect, of EU data protection law can apply to the relevant scheme. If they are successful in their application, they earn the right to display the relevant badge or emblem.

Seals and certifications last for a relatively brief period of three years, after which a renewal is necessary. Consequently, seal and certification schemes result in an ongoing, burdensome and potentially expensive process.

Article 43: Certification Bodies

Enforcement of seal or certification schemes

A seal or certification scheme only has value if it demonstrates compliance with EU data protection law. Therefore, it must be overseen and enforced, in order to ensure that it achieves that aim.

Art.42(5), 43(2)

Seal and certification schemes are overseen and enforced, either by the relevant DPA, or an independent body which has an appropriate level of expertise in relation to data protection and has been accredited by the relevant DPA. An independent body may be appointed to this role for a maximum of five years if it is:

- *independent and has demonstrated its expertise;*
- *has established procedures for issuing, reviewing and withdrawing seals or certifications;*
- *has established procedures for dealing with complaints or infringements of the seals or certifications; and*

- *can demonstrate that it has no conflicts of interest in this role.*

Such a body may be appointed to monitor compliance with a seal or certification scheme and withdraw the seal or certification if its requirements are no longer met. DPAs still retain their own separate enforcement powers.

Organisations that wish to obtain a seal or certification are subject to enforcement by the DPA or independent body that oversees the relevant seal or certification scheme.

Chapter 5: Transfer of personal data to third countries of international organizations

In This Chapter we will cover the following Articles:

Article 44: General Principle for transfer
Article 45: Transfers of the basis of an adequacy decision
Article 46: Transfers subject to appropriate safeguards
Article 47: Binding corporate rules
Article 48: Transfers or disclosures not authorised by union law
Article 49: Derogations for specific situations
Article 50: International cooperation for the protection of personal data

In today's world, it is increasingly important to be able to move data freely to wherever those data are needed. However, the transfer of personal data to recipients outside the EEA is generally prohibited unless:

- the jurisdiction in which the recipient is located is deemed to provide an adequate level of data protection;
- the data exporter puts in place appropriate safeguards; or

- a derogation or exemption applies.

Understanding the application of lawful data transfer mechanisms is essential for all organisations that wish to transfer personal data to recipients located outside the EEA (including processors, such as cloud service providers).

Article 44: General Principle for transfer

General prohibition on transfers

Cross-Border Data Transfers are prohibited, unless certain conditions are met.

Art.44, 45

Cross-Border Data Transfers may only take place if the transfer is made to an Adequate Jurisdiction (see below) or the data exporter has implemented a lawful data transfer mechanism (or an exemption or derogation applies).

The GDPR and the Directive have essentially similar general restrictions on Cross-Border Data Transfers.

Commission Adequacy Decisions

Cross-Border Data Transfers to a recipient in a third country may take place, without a need to obtain any further authorisation, if the Commission has decided that such third country ensures an adequate level of data protection (an "Adequate Jurisdiction"). The basis for this principle is that such jurisdictions provide sufficient protection for the rights and freedoms of data subjects without the need for further safeguards.

The current list of Adequate Jurisdictions is: Andorra, Argentina, Canada (for organisations that are subject to Canada's PIPEDA law), Switzerland, the Faeroe Islands, Guernsey, Israel, Isle of Man, Jersey, New Zealand, and Uruguay. Following the decision in *Schrems*, the US-EU Safe Harbour is no longer deemed adequate. It has effectively been replaced by the EU-US Privacy Shield.

Art.44, 45

Cross-Border Data Transfers to a recipient in a third country may take place if the third country receives an Adequacy Decision from the Commission. Factors that may affect an Adequacy Decision include, inter alia:

- *the rule of law and legal protections for human rights and fundamental freedoms;*
- *access to transferred data by public authorities;*
- *existence and effective functioning of DPAs; and*
- *international commitments and other obligations in relation to the protection of personal data.*

The Commission may declare third countries (or a territory, a specified sector, or an international organisation) to be Adequate Jurisdictions.

Existing Adequacy Decisions adopted by the Commission where on the basis of the current Directive so they remain in force only until the time they are amended, replaced or repealed in accordance with the GDPR. The attributes of the 'adequacy requirements' is more detailed under the GDPR so it is unclear whether further countries will qualify, or even whether existing countries will maintain their status, as Adequate Jurisdictions.

Article 45: Transfers of the basis of an adequacy decision

Review of Adequacy Decisions

The Commission's Adequacy Decisions may need to be reviewed from time to time, especially as they may meet judicial challenge as illustrated by the *Schrems* decision. Therefore, it is always possible that conditions in an Adequate Jurisdiction may change, and that jurisdiction may no longer provide adequate protection.

Art.45(3)-(5), 93(2)-(3)

Adequacy Decisions are subject to a periodic review, at least every four years, taking into account all relevant developments. The Commission can repeal, amend or suspend Adequacy Decisions for jurisdictions no longer ensuring an adequate level of data protection (without retro-active effect).

Under the GDPR, any Adequacy Decisions made remain valid for a maximum of 4 years and may be amended, suspended or repealed. This may affect the ability of organisations to rely on Adequacy Decisions in the long-term.

Article 46: Transfers subject to appropriate safeguards

Agreements between public authorities

Public sector Cross-Border Data Transfers may take place on the basis of agreements between a public authority in the EU and a public authority in a third country, without requiring a specific authorisation from a DPA.

Art.46(2)(a), (3)(b)

Cross-Border Data Transfers between public authorities may take place on the basis of agreements between public authorities, which do not require any specific authorisation from a DPA. The public authorities must ensure compliance with GDPR requirements.

Private organisations that are dealing with international regulatory investigations may benefit from the ability of national public authorities to lawfully transfer data between themselves on this basis.

Model Clauses

Cross-Border Data Transfers may take place on the basis of standard data protection clauses approved by the Commission ('Model Clauses').

Art.28(6)-(8), 46(2)(c), 57(1)(j), (r), 93(2)

Cross-Border Data Transfers are permitted if the controller or processor adduces appropriate safeguards in the form of Model Clauses. These do not require any further authorisation from a DPA. The Commission may create new types of Model Clauses.

Under the GDPR the DPA no longer needs to authorise data transfers made under the Model Clauses. In addition, any existing Model Clauses implemented under the Directive remain valid until amended, replaced or repealed in accordance with the GDPR.

DPA Clauses

Cross-Border Data Transfers may take place on the basis of standard data protection clauses adopted by one or more DPAs, in accordance with the GDPR ("DPA Clauses").

Art.46(2)(d), 64(1)(d), 57(1)(j), (r), 93(2)

A Cross-Border Data Transfer may take place on the basis of DPA Clauses, which offer a national alternative to the Commission-approved Model Clauses. Transfers made on the basis of DPA Clauses do not require further DPA approval. DPA Clauses may be included in a wider contract (e.g., from one processor to another), provided the original wording of the authorised DPA Clauses is not contradicted (directly or indirectly).

The GDPR introduces DPA Clauses in a bid to prevent organisations from forum-shopping. DPA Clauses might develop in a similar direction as Model Clauses which are an established and proven concept.

Codes of Conduct

A Cross-Border Data Transfer may take place on the basis of approved Codes of Conduct.

Art.40, 41, 46(2)(e)

A Cross-Border Data Transfer may take place on the basis of an approved Code of Conduct, together with binding and enforceable commitments to provide appropriate safeguards. Transfers made on this basis do not require DPA approval.

The GDPR introduces the possibility of Cross-Border Data Transfers made in reliance on approved Codes of Conduct. This permits organisations greater flexibility in selecting the data transfer mechanisms that best suit their needs.

Certification

A Cross-Border Data Transfer may take place on the basis of certifications.

Art.42, 43, 46(2)(f)

A Cross-Border Data Transfer may take place on the basis of certifications together with binding and enforceable commitments of the data importer to apply the certification to the transferred data. Transfers made on this basis do not require DPA approval (although, as set out <u>in Chapter 12</u>, the certification scheme itself requires DPA approval).

The GDPR introduces certifications as a new lawful mechanism for Cross-Border Data Transfers. This permits organisations greater flexibility in selecting the data transfer mechanisms that best suit their needs.

Ad hoc clauses

A Cross-Border Data Transfer may take place on the basis of contracts negotiated between the data exporter and the data importer ("ad hoc clauses"), subject to approval from the competent DPA.

Art.46(3)(a), (4), 63

A Cross-Border Data Transfer may take place on the basis of ad hoc clauses. These clauses must conform to the requirements of the GDPR, and must be approved by the relevant DPA subject to the Consistency Mechanism, before transfers can begin.

The Directive and the GDPR both permit Cross Border Data Transfers made on the basis of ad hoc clauses. Existing DPA approvals of ad hoc clauses remain valid until amended, replaced or repealed in accordance with the GDPR. DPAs are obliged to apply the Consistency Mechanism which will, in theory, ensure a consistent regulatory approach across all Member States.

Administrative arrangements

A Cross-Border Data Transfer may take place on the basis of administrative arrangements made by the data exporter, subject to the authorisation from the competent DPA.

Art.46(3)(b), (4), 63

Cross-Border Data Transfers may take place on the basis of administrative arrangements between public authorities (e.g., a Memorandum of Understanding), which include adequate protection for the rights of data subjects. Transfers made on this basis require DPA approval.

Private organisations that are dealing with regulatory investigations may benefit from the ability of national public authorities to lawfully transfer data between themselves on this basis.

Article 47: Binding corporate rules

Binding Corporate Rules

Cross-Border Data Transfer within a corporate group may take place on the basis of Binding Corporate Rules ("BCRs"). The BCRs require approval from DPAs, but once such approval is obtained, individual transfers made under the BCRs do not require further approval

Art.4(20) 46(2)(b), 47

The GDPR directly addresses the concept of BCRs. The competent DPA will approve BCRs as an appropriate mechanism for Cross-Border Data Transfers within a corporate group (including to members of that group that are established in third countries). If the BCRs meet the requirements set out in the GDPR, they will be approved, and no further DPA approval will be required for transfers of personal data made under the BCRs.

The GDPR unlike the Directive explicitly recognises and encourages BCRs and provides clear provisions on requirements and procedures for using BCRs. This significant change in outlook is likely to make it easier for organisations to obtain DPA approval for, and implement, BCRs.

Content of BCRs

Although the language of BCRs can be drafted by the parties, that language must cover certain specified topics, and satisfy the requirements of EU data protection law, before the BCRs can be approved by DPAs.

Art.47(1)-(3)

BCRs must include a mechanism to make the BCRs legally binding on group companies. Among other things, the BCRs must:

- *specify the purposes of the transfer and affected categories of data;*
- *reflect the requirements of the GDPR;*
- *confirm that the EU-based data exporters accept liability on behalf of the entire group;*
- *explain complaint procedures; and*
- *provide mechanisms for ensuring compliance (e.g., audits).*

The GDPR provides specific guidance on the criteria that BCRs must cover in order to meet compliance. Therefore if the BCR complies with this list of criteria, businesses can significantly increase the likelihood of obtaining DPA approval for their BCRs.

Approval of BCRs

Unlike Model Clauses the content of BCRs can be drafted to suit the needs and circumstances of the organisation. Consequently BCRs are not deemed to be pre-approved. Instead, BCRs always require prior approval from DPAs.

Art.47(1), 57(1)(s)

The competent DPA must approve BCRs that fulfil the criteria set out in the GDPR. Where the BCRs are intended to cover data transfers from multiple Member States, the Consistency Mechanism applies.

The fact that approval must be given by the competent DPA for compliant BCRs is likely to make the adoption of BCRs easier and should significantly decrease the inconsistencies in the interpretation and implementation of BCRs from one DPA to another. Existing approvals of BCRs created under the Directive remain valid until amended, replaced or repealed in accordance with the GDPR.

Article 48: Transfers or disclosures not authorised by union law

Third country judgments and decisions

Third country court judgments, or administrative authority decisions, are recognised as a lawful basis for a Cross-Border Data Transfer only if the transfer is subject to appropriate international agreements.

Art.48

A judgment from a third country, requiring a Cross-Border Data Transfer, only provides a lawful basis for such a transfer if the transfer is based on an appropriate international agreement, such as a Mutual Legal Assistance Treaty. However, this is without prejudice to other grounds for a transfer.

This requirement may result in organisations being unable to comply with orders from courts in third countries (e.g., the US) without the existence of an appropriate international agreement. If no such agreement exists, the transfer may nevertheless be lawful if the conditions of Art.45, 46, 47 or 48 are met.

Article 49: Derogations for specific situations

Consent

A Cross-Border Data Transfer may be made on the basis of the consent of the data subject.

Art.49(1)(a), (3)

A Cross-Border Data Transfer may be made on the basis that the data subject, having been informed of the possible risks of such transfer, explicitly consents

Although in practical purposes the change from "unambiguous" consent to "explicit" consent is unlikely to have any significant impact for most organisations. The obligation to prove that data subjects have been informed of the possible risks associated with the transfer may well prove to be a more troublesome challenge. Indeed it will impose a material administrative burden on organisations that rely on consent as a lawful basis for Cross-Border Data Transfers.

Contracts between a data subject and a controller

A Cross-Border Data Transfer may be made on the basis that it is necessary for the purposes of performing or implementing a contract between the data subject and the controller.

Art.49(1)(b), (3)

A Cross-Border Data Transfer may take place if the transfer is necessary for:

- *the performance of a contract between the data subject and the controller; or*
- *the implementation of pre-contractual measures taken in response to the data subject's request.*

The position under the Directive is essentially unchanged under the GDPR.

Contracts that are in the data subject's interest

A Cross-Border Data Transfer may be made on the basis that it is necessary for the purposes of performing or concluding a contract in the interests of the data subject (e.g., a parent making a purchase on behalf of a child).

Art.49(1)(c), (3)

A Cross-Border Data Transfer may take place if the transfer is necessary for the conclusion or performance of a contract between the controller and a third party, where it is in the interests of the data subject.

Public interest

A Cross-Border Data Transfer may be made on the basis that the transfer is necessary for important reasons of public interest.

Art.49(1)(d), (4)

A Cross-Border Data Transfer may take place if the transfer is necessary for important reasons of public interest. Such interests must be recognised in EU law or in the law of the Member State to which the controller is subject.

The changes introduced by the GDPR make little practical difference, because interests that are not recognised by EU or Member State law are unlikely to be viewed by DPAs as a lawful basis for a Cross Border Data Transfer.

Legal claims

A Cross-Border Data Transfer may be made on the basis that it is necessary for the purposes of legal proceedings, or obtaining legal advice.

Art.49(1)(e)

A Cross-Border Data Transfer may take place if the transfer is necessary for the establishment, exercise or defence of legal claims.

Data subject's vital interests

A Cross-Border Data Transfer may be made on the basis that the transfer is necessary to protect the vital interests of the data subject.

Art.49(1)(f)

A Cross-Border Data Transfer may take place if the transfer is necessary in order to protect the vital interests of the data subject or of other persons, where the data subject is physically or legally incapable of giving consent.

Extending the scope of this ground to cover third parties provides organisations with another lawful basis for Cross-Border Data Transfers, albeit in limited circumstances. In reality, very few organisations will ever make use of this basis for Cross-Border Data Transfers, as this basis only justifies transfers in a "life-or-death" situation.

Public registers

A Cross-Border Data Transfer may be made on the basis that the data to be transferred are taken from a public register.

Art.49(1)(g), (2)

A Cross-Border Data Transfer may take place if the transferred data are taken from a register which is open to the public or, upon request, to any person who can demonstrate a legitimate interest in inspecting it. This does not permit a transfer of the entire register.

Controller's compelling legitimate interests

A Cross-Border Data Transfer may be made on the basis that the transfer is necessary for the purposes of a compelling legitimate interests of the controller.

Art.49(1), (3), (6)

A Cross-Border Data Transfer may take place if:

- *none of the other lawful bases applies;*
- *the transfer is not repetitive;*
- *it only concerns a limited number of data subjects;*
- *the transfer is necessary for the purposes of compelling legitimate interests pursued by the controller which are not overridden by those of the data subject; and*
- *the controller has adduced suitable safeguards for the transferred data.*

The controller must inform the relevant DPA and the data subjects about the transfer.

The GDPR introduces the possibility that organisations may be able to make Cross-Border Data Transfers on the basis of compelling legitimate interests. Even if the scope of this transfer mechanism is narrow, it provides for another option to enable Cross-Border Data Transfers.

Certain transfer mechanisms may be limited by law

A number of lawful mechanisms for Cross-Border Data Transfers may be limited, under applicable EU or Member State law, to certain categories of data.

Art.49(5)

EU law or law of the Member States may, for important reasons of public interest, expressly limits Cross–Border Data Transfers relating to specific categories of personal data. Member States must notify such restrictions to the Commission.

The fact that individual Member States can restrict the ability of organisations to transfer certain categories of personal data may severely hamper the business activities of some organisations, and result in inconsistent restrictions from one Member State to the next.

Article 50: International cooperation for the protection of personal data

International and Third Party Cooperation

"... develop international cooperation mechanisms to facilitate the effective enforcement of legislation for the protection of personal data;

Under GDPR will strive to establish mutual assistance with international third parties for the purpose of:

b) provide international mutual assistance in the enforcement of legislation for the protection of personal data, including through notification, complaint referral, investigative assistance and information exchange, subject to appropriate safeguards for the protection of personal data and other fundamental rights and freedoms;

The GDPR takes a more cohesive approach to forming mutual assistance agreements rather than leaving it up to individual national authorities.

Chapter 6: Independent Supervisory Authorities

In this Chapter we will cover the following Articles:

Section 1: Independent status
Article 51: Supervisory Authority

Article 52: Independence
Article 53: General conditions for the members of the supervisory authority
Article 54: Rules on the establishment of the supervisory Authority

Section 2: Competence, Tasks, and Powers
Article 55: Competence
Article 56: Competence of the lead supervisory authority
Article 57: Tasks
Article 58: Powers
Article 59: Activity Reports

National Data Protection Authorities ("DPAs") are appointed to implement and enforce data protection law, and to offer guidance. DPAs have significant enforcement powers, including the ability to issue substantial fines. Understanding the role and responsibilities of DPAs is vital to achieving compliance.

Section 1: Independent status

DPAs are responsible for enforcing EU data protection law. They (together with the Working Party 29/EDPB) also provide guidance on the interpretation of that law. While such guidance from the WP29 is not legally binding, it is likely to be in accord with the interpretation of the law held by the DPA and hence indicative of the enforcement position.

DPAs are appointed by each Member State although some Member States do appoint multiple DPAs in a federal structure i.e. Germany. Other member States appoint separate public bodies with specific responsibility for enforcing different aspects of data protection law.

However, most organisations are not likely to have a relationship with a DPA and their only contact is likely to be when a complaint has been raised against them, they have experienced a serious breach has occurred. Dealing with DPAs should not be taken as a trivial matter, and it is important for an organisation to ensure that it has legal advisors to hand who are experienced, knowledgeable and familiar with the operations of DPAs.

Article 51: Supervisory Authority

Responsibilities of DPAs

DPAs are responsible for enforcing data protection laws at a national level, and providing guidance on the interpretation of those laws.

Art.51

Each Member State is required to appoint one or more DPAs to implement the Regulation and protect the rights and freedoms of individuals.

The primary roles and responsibilities of the DPAs have not significantly change under the GDPR. Organisations can largely rely on their existing experience of interactions with DPAs.

Jurisdiction

Each DPA is appointed at a national level, through national legislation. Its jurisdiction and enforcement powers are largely restricted to the territory of its own Member State.

Art.51, 55, 56

Each DPA can only exercise its powers on the territory of its own Member State but, under the "One-Stop-Shop" (see below); the DPA's regulatory actions may affect processing that occurs in other Member States.

Organisations that operate across multiple Member States will face a new set of challenges in their interactions with DPAs. Organisations that operate only within a single Member State, and only process personal data of residents of that Member State, will be largely unaffected.

Article 52: Independence

Independence

DPAs must be free from all outside influences, including government control.

Art.52

Each DPA must act with complete independence in carrying out its functions.

The GDPR essentially replicates the requirements set out in the Directive, albeit in greater detail.

Article 53: General conditions for the members of the supervisory authority

Establishment and appointment of DPAs

In order to ensure that DPAs apply and enforce EU data protection law in a fair, uniform and impartial manner, certain minimum requirements must be met in terms of their establishment and appointment.

Art.53-54

Each DPA must:

- *be created through a transparent procedure;*
- *have the skills and experience necessary to perform the role; and*
- *be subject to a duty of professional secrecy.*

Article 54: Rules on the establishment of the supervisory Authority

Establishment of the Supervisory Authority

For the establishment of each supervisory authority each Member State shall provide by law;

Act 54

"the qualifications and eligibility conditions required to be appointed as member of each supervisory authority;"

The GDPR establishes that the Member State the rules and procedures for the appointment of the member or members of each supervisory authority;

Section 2: Competence, Tasks, and Powers

Article 55: Competence

The "One-Stop-Shop"

The concept of the One-Stop-Shop is to provide a single, uniform decision-making process in the scenario where an organization may be established in several Member States in which case multiple regulators may claim responsibility for regulating the same activity performed by the same organisation in different Member States. The aim of the One-Stop-Shop is to provide a single Lead Authority and point of contact.

Art.55-56

If an organisation has establishments in multiple Member States, the DPA for its "main establishment" (i.e., the place where its main processing decisions are taken) will be its "lead authority". This lead authority has the power to regulate that organisation across all Member States (to the extent its data processing activities involve cross-border data processing).

The "One-Stop-Shop" will mean greater harmonisation, and the more uniform application of EU data protection law, as an organisation will generally deal with a single lead DPA.

Article 56: Competence of the lead supervisory authority

Article 57: Tasks

Tasks of DPAs

DPAs are required to perform certain tasks, including monitoring and enforcement of EU data protection law.

Art.55, 57

The tasks of DPAs include obligations to:

- *monitor and enforce the application of the GDPR;*
- *promote awareness of the risks, rules, safeguards and rights pertaining to personal data (especially in relation to children);*
- *advise national and governmental institutions on the application of the GDPR;*
- *hear claims brought by data subjects or their representatives, and inform data subjects of the outcome of such claims;*
- *establish requirements for Impact Assessments;*
- *encourage the creation of Codes of Conduct and review certifications;*
- *authorise Model Clauses and BCRs;*
- *keep records of sanctions and enforcement actions and*
- *fulfil "any other tasks related to protection of personal data".*

The tasks of DPAs are significantly more broadly defined in the GDPR than in the Directive.

Article 58: Powers

Powers of DPAs

DPAs have the power to enforce data protection laws at a national level.

Art.58

DPAs are empowered to oversee enforcement of the GDPR, investigate breaches of the GDPR and bring legal proceedings where necessary.

The legal powers of DPAs are largely unchanged. At a practical level, it is likely that there will continue to be some variation between the practical enforcement powers available to DPAs, due to variations in the national laws of Member States.

Article 59: Activity Reports

Activity reports

In order to ensure fairness and transparency, DPAs are required to draw up and publish regular reports explaining their activities.

Art.59

Each DPA must draw up an annual report on its activities. The report must be made available to the public.

Chapter 7: Co-operation and Consistency

In this Chapter we cover the following Articles:

Section 1: Co-operation
Article 60: Cooperation between the lead supervisory authority and the other supervisory authorities concerned
Article 61: Mutual Assistance
Article 62: Joint operations of supervisory authorities

Section 2: Consistency
Article 63: Consistency mechanism
Article 64: Opinion of the Board
Article 65: Dispute resolution by the Board
Article 66: Urgency Procedure
Article 67: Exchange of information

Section 3: European Data Protection Board (IS NOT COVERED)
Article 68: European Data Protection Board
Article 69: Independence
Article 70: Tasks of the Board
Article 71: Reports
Article 72: Procedure
Article 73: Chair
Article 74: Tasks of the Chair

Article 75: Secretariat
Article 76: Confidentiality

Section 1: Co-operation

Article 60: Cooperation between the lead supervisory authority and the other supervisory authorities concerned

DPA cooperation

In order for EU data protection law to operate consistently across all Member States, it is important for DPAs to cooperate with one another

Article 61: Mutual Assistance

Art.61-62

DPAs are required to cooperate and provide each other with mutual assistance. They also have formal legal authority to carry out joint operations.

In cases in which organisations are under investigation in multiple Member States, these changes should make the investigation process easier to manage.

Article 62: Joint operations of supervisory authorities

Section 2: Consistency

Article 63: Consistency mechanism

The Consistency Mechanism

One of the most significant difficulties organisations face in dealing with DPAs is the inconsistent nature of decisions taken at the national level.

Art.4(23), 56, 63-67

Where an organisation engages in cross-border data processing (i.e., processing that affects data subjects in multiple Member States), a DPA that wishes to take action must consult with the other affected DPAs to ensure consistency in the application of the GDPR.

For any organisation that operates in multiple Member States, the Consistency Mechanism is a positive development, as it should result in a more uniform application of EU data protection law.

The Consistency Mechanism

Where a DPA takes a decision that only affects the processing of personal data on the territory of its own Member State (e.g., where an organisation only operates within that Member State) the Consistency Mechanism does not apply. However, where a DPA takes a decision affecting processing across multiple Member States, that decision must be notified to the EDPB, which must then produce an opinion on the decision within 8 weeks (extended to 14 weeks in complex cases).

In principle, the Consistency Mechanism is an encouraging approach to ensuring that organisations where ever they do business will have fair and consistent compliance requirements across the Member States in which they are established. In practice however, organisations and data subjects have no direct input into the Consistency Mechanism, and this will reduce the transparency of the process.

Art.63, 64(2)

DPAs across all Member States are required to co-operate with each other and with the EDPB and the Commission, to ensure consistent application of the GDPR.

The GDPR makes it mandatory for national DPAs to cooperate and where cases have an impact in more than one Member State they may be referred to the EDPB. This process should help to ensure that organisations face more consistent compliance requirements across the EU.

Article 64: Opinion of the Board

Opinion of the EDPB

Even if the applicable national data protection laws set similar standards across all Member States, enforcement requirements, attitudes, and standards may vary from Member State to Member State. Ensuring similar enforcement standards is a core issue for EU data protection law.

Art.64

DPAs must submit a draft to the EDPB before taking any of the following measures:

- *specifying processing measures that should be subject to an Impact Assessment;*
- *approving a Code of Conduct;*
- *approving accreditation criteria;*
- *determining the content of DPA Clauses;*
- *authorising ad hoc; or*
- *approving BCRs.*

DPAs are required to submit to the EDPB decisions that are likely to affect data subjects or organisations in multiple Member States. This is to ensure that DPAs take consistent decisions across Member States, in order to provide a consistent application of the law across the EU.

The task for the EDPB will be to examine each case or measure where the matter in question affects multiple Member States and issue an opinion. The relevant DPA must take "utmost account" of the EDPB's opinion in proceeding with its decision. The downside of course is that it can introduce needless delays by involving the EDPB as a new step in the decision-making process.

Article 65: Dispute resolution by the Board

Dispute resolution by the EDPB

Where there is disagreement between national DPAs there is a potential risk of inconsistent application of data protection law across the EU. By allowing a central authority to make binding decisions reduces this risk.

Art.65

Where DPAs disagree about key data protection law issues, the EDPB will issue a binding decision, which must then be adopted by the Concerned DPA(s) within one month of notification of the EDPB's decision.

Article 66: Urgency Procedure

Urgency procedure

One drawback of requiring DPAs to refer enforcement issues to a central authority is that this may lead to delays. In many cases, the delay might not prejudice the outcome of the proceedings, but there is a risk that, in some cases, it may do so. Therefore, there is a need to allow for more rapid decisions in cases of urgency.

Art.66

Where a DPA considers there to be an urgent need to act to protect data subjects' rights, it may immediately adopt provisional measures for up to three months. A full explanation should be provided to other Concerned DPAs, the EDPB and the Commission. Urgent opinions may also be requested from the EDPB

Article 67: Exchange of information

Exchange of information

In order to ensure that EU data protection law is applied consistently, it is important to ensure that DPAs and the EDPB are communicating clearly.

Art.47(3), 50, 60(1), 61(3), (9), 67, 70(c), (u)-(w)

The Commission may implement acts which specify arrangements for electronic exchange of information between DPAs and the EDPB. The EDPB may advise on these issues.

This provision is designed to ensure a free flow of information between concerned DPAs and the EDPB.

Oversight by the EDPB

Because the EDPB does not yet exist, and because the provisions governing the Consistency Mechanism and oversight by the EDPB are not effective yet, it is unclear how the EDPB will fulfil its role in resolving disputes between DPAs. Current practice indicates that there are likely to be many cases in which DPAs have different opinions about the correct application of EU data protection law (see, for example, the significantly divergent views of DPAs following the CJEU's decision in *Schrems*). Where DPAs disagree, the EDPB may be called in to adjudicate under Art.64. Given the potentially high numbers of disagreements, and the length of time it may take for DPAs and the EDPB to familiarise themselves with this mechanism, there may be delays until the EDPB's processes work smoothly.

Section 3: European Data Protection Board

Article 68 – European Data Protection Board

The European Data Protection Board (the 'Board') is hereby established as a body of the Union and shall have legal personality.

2. The Board shall be represented by its Chair.

3. The Board shall be composed of the head of one supervisory authority of each Member State and of the European Data Protection Supervisor or their respective representatives.

Under the GDPR the Board now replaces the Working Party on the Protection of Individuals which sat under the Directive.

Article 69 – Independence

Independence of the Board

The Board will act independently and without prejudice to requests by the Commission

Act 69

The Board shall act independently when performing its tasks or exercising its powers pursuant to Articles 70 and 71

Article 70 –Tasks of the Board

Tasks of the Board

Amongst many other review and recommendation functions the Boards tasks are to:

Art 70

Monitor and ensure the correct application of this Regulation in the cases provided for in Articles 64 and 65 without prejudice to the tasks of national supervisory authorities;

(b) advise the Commission on any issue related to the protection of personal data in the Union, including on any proposed amendment of this Regulation;

(c) advise the Commission on the format and procedures for the exchange of information between controllers, processors and supervisory authorities for binding corporate rules;

(d) issue guidelines, recommendations, and best practices on procedures and offer advice to the Commission

Article 71- Reports

Reporting Duties

Art-71

The Board shall draw up an annual report regarding the protection of natural persons with regard to processing in the Union and, where relevant, in third countries and international organisations.

Article 72- Procedure

Board Procedures

The Board shall take decisions by a simple majority of its members, unless otherwise provided for in this Regulation.

Art 72

The Board shall adopt its own rules of procedure by a two-thirds majority of its members and organise its own operational arrangements.

Article 73- Chair

Terms of Office of the Chair

The Board shall elect a Chair and two deputies.

Act 73

The Board shall elect a chair and two deputy chairs from amongst its members by simple majority. The term of office of the Chair and of the deputy chairs shall be five years and be renewable once.

Activity 74 – Tasks of the Chair

Tasks of the Chair

The Board shall lay down the allocation of tasks between the Chair and the deputy chairs in its rules of procedure. But the general tasks outlined by the GDPR are:

Act 74

to convene the meetings of the Board and prepare its agenda;

(b) to notify decisions adopted by the Board pursuant to Article 65 to the lead supervisory authority and the supervisory authorities concerned;

(c) to ensure the timely performance of the tasks of the Board, in particular in relation to the consistency mechanism referred to in Article 63.

Article 75 – Secretariat

Board Secretariat

The Board shall have a secretariat, which shall be provided by the European Data Protection Supervisor.

Act 75

The secretariat shall provide analytical, administrative and logistical support to the Board.

Activity 76 – Confidentiality

Confidentiality

The discussions of the Board shall be confidential where the Board deems it necessary, as provided for in its rules of procedure.

Act 76

Access to documents submitted to members of the Board, experts and representatives of third parties shall be governed by Regulation (EC) No 1049/2001 of the European Parliament and of the Council

Chapter 8: Remedies, Liability, and Sanctions

In this Chapter we cover the following Articles:

Article 77: Right to lodge a complaint with a supervisory authority
Article 78: Right to an effective judicial remedy against a supervisory authority
Article 79: Right to an effective judicial remedy against a controller or processor
Article 80: Representation of data subjects
Article 81: Suspension of proceedings
Article 82: Right to compensation and liability
Article 83: General conditions for imposing administrative fines
Article 84: Penalties

Whereas the remedies and sanctions available to DPAs under the Directive are comparatively low (generally subject to a maximum of less than €1 million per infringement, with average fines being in the low tens of thousands) the remedies and sanctions available to DPAs under the GDPR are significantly greater. In particular, the GDPR allows DPAs to issue fines for serious infringements up to a maximum of the greater of €20 million or four percent of worldwide turnover.

The GDPR sets out new maximum fines of the greater of €20 million or four percent of an undertaking's worldwide turnover. This is arguably the most significant single change set out in the GDPR, and is likely to cause organisations to view compliance with EU data protection law in a fundamentally different way.

The GDPR also provides that DPAs must take into account a range of factors when deciding whether to impose a fine, and what the amount of that fine should be. It is hoped that this approach will result in a more uniform approach by DPAs to the significant fines introduced under the GDPR.

Article 77: Right to lodge a complaint with a supervisory authority

Right to complain to a DPA

Data subjects', who believe that their rights have been infringed, have the right to ask the data controller to remedy the situation. If the complainant does not receive an adequate response, the data subject can escalate the complaint to the relevant national DPA.

Art.77

Data Subjects have the right to lodge complaints concerning the processing of his or her personal data with a DPA in the Member State in which they live or work, or the Member State in which the alleged infringement occurred. The DPA is required to keep the data subject informed on the progress and the outcome of the complaint.

The GDPR clarifies the fact that data subjects can complain to different DPAs, depending on where they live or work, or where the alleged infringement took place. However, under the "One-Stop-Shop" the DPA to which the complaint is addressed may not necessarily be the one that acts upon the complaint.

Article 78: Right to an effective judicial remedy against a supervisory authority

Right to a judicial remedy

If the data subject is not satisfied with the DPA's response to their complaint, the data subject is entitled to escalate the complaint before a national court.

Art.78-79

Data subjects have the right to an effective judicial remedy against:

- *decisions of a DPA concerning them;*
- *any failure by a DPA to deal with, or respond to, a complaint within three months; and*
- *Any unlawful processing of their personal data by a controller or processor.*

Article 79: Right to an effective judicial remedy against a controller or processor

Venue for proceedings

The question of which courts have authority to hear a particular claim frequently arises when a data subject in one Member State might be affected by processing activities taking place in another Member State.

Art.78(3), 79(2)

Proceedings against a DPA or public authority must be brought in the Member State in which the DPA is established.

Proceedings against a controller or processor may be brought in:

- *the Member State in which the controller or processor has an establishment; or*

- *the Member State in which the data subject resides (except to the extent that the controller or processor is a DPA or public authority).*

Article 80: Representation of data subjects

Representation of data subjects

A data subject may be represented in the exercise of their rights by representatives who, under national law, fulfil the necessary requirements.

Art.80

A not-for-profit body, organisation or association whose statutory objectives are in the public interest and which is active in the field of the protection of data subjects' rights and freedoms may lodge a complaint to a DPA on behalf of a data subject or exercise the right to judicial remedy and the right to seek compensation on behalf of data subjects. Under national law, Member States may mandate a body to lodge complaints on behalf of data subjects, without being mandated by those data subjects.

The GDPR clarifies the requirements regarding claims brought by third parties on behalf of data subjects for example a Union Official or a Legal Representative. The GDPR also allows for the possibility of representatives seeking judicial remedies and compensation from organisations, on behalf of multiple data subjects. (Class Actions)

Article 81: Suspension of proceedings

Suspension of proceedings

In an increasingly internationalised world, it is not uncommon for judicial proceedings to be brought in multiple jurisdictions regarding the same subject matter.

Art.81

Where a court in one Member State learns of proceedings pending in another Member State, concerning the same controller or processor and the same subject matter, that court may:

- *contact the relevant court in the other Member State to confirm the existence of such proceedings; and*
- *suspend its own proceedings if appropriate.*

Where these proceedings are pending at first instance, any other court may also, on the application of one of the parties, decline jurisdiction, if the court first seized has jurisdiction.

The GDPR lessens the burden on organisations that are faced with parallel proceedings in multiple Member States by allowing national courts to suspend proceedings. However it is possible that claims could be delayed if a national court decides to suspend proceedings pending the outcome of a case in another Member State.

Article 82: Right to compensation and liability

Compensation and liability

EU data protection law takes the view that controllers and processors should be liable to pay compensation to data subjects in the event of any unlawful processing of personal data.

Art.82(1)-(2), (4)

A data subject who has suffered harm as a result of the unlawful processing of his or her personal data has the right to receive compensation from the controller or processor for the harm suffered.

- *Any controller involved in the processing is liable for the harm caused.*

- *A processor is liable for the harm caused by any of its (or its sub-processor's) processing activities that are not in compliance with its obligations under the GDPR, or are in breach of the controller's instructions.*
- *To ensure effective compensation, each controller or processor will be held liable for the entirety of the harm caused, if they are involved in the same processing and responsible for that harm.*

The GDPR expands the scope of liability for infringements of EU data protection law to both controllers and processors.

Liability of joint controllers

The question of how liability should be apportioned between joint controllers, while important to organisations, is not of primary concern from the perspective of EU data protection law their primacy is with ensuring the protection of the data subject.

Art.26(3), 82(3)-(5)

Data subjects are entitled to enforce their rights against any of the joint controllers. Each joint controller is liable for the entirety of the damage, although national law may apportion liability between them. If one joint controller has paid full compensation, it may then bring proceedings against the other joint controllers to recover their portions of the damages.

The GDPR makes joint controllers fully liable. Once "full compensation" has been paid to the affected data subject(s), joint controllers may recover damages from one another. This means that some joint controllers may find themselves facing much higher liability for claims made under the GDPR.

Exemptions from liability

In line with general principles of liability, a controller or processor is exempt from liability to the extent that it is not responsible for the relevant harm.

Art.82(3)

A controller or processor is exempt from liability if it proves that it is not responsible for the event giving rise to the harm. There is no mention of force majeure events.

The GDPR creates the possibility of direct liability for controllers and it therefore extends this exemption to processors. In all other respects, this principle remains unchanged under the GDPR. However a significant change is that the Directive exempts controllers from liability for harm arising in cases of force majeure. The GDPR contains no such exemption, meaning that controllers may bear the risk in force majeure cases.

Article 83: General conditions for imposing administrative fines

Administrative fines

As is common in other areas of regulatory law, a system of penalties and administrative fines exists to ensure compliance with the requirements of EU data protection law.

Art.83

Each DPA shall ensure that it imposes sanctions and administrative fines in a manner that is effective, proportionate and dissuasive.

Where a Member State's legal system does not provide for administrative fines, fines may be initiated by the DPA and imposed by the national courts.

The concept of administrative fines for breaches of EU data protection law changes only very slightly under the GDPR. However, there are significant changes to both the amount of any fines and the factors relevant to determining those fines.

Maximum administrative fines

As with many other areas of regulatory law, EU data protection law has a concept of a maximum fine, in order to help ensure that fines are applied on a broadly consistent and proportionate scale.

Art.83(5)-(6)

The maximum fine that can be imposed for serious infringements of the GDPR is the greater of €20 million or four percent of an undertaking's worldwide turnover for the preceding financial year.

The GDPR sets out new maximum fines of the greater of €20 million or four percent of an undertaking's worldwide turnover, fundamentally changing the potential financial consequences of breaching EU data protection law.

Application of administrative fines by DPAs

The issue of how DPAs determine whether to issue a fine and, if so, what the amount of that fine should be, is fundamental to ensuring the consistent application of EU data protection law.

Art.83(2)

When deciding whether to impose a fine and deciding on the amount, DPAs are required to give due regard to a range of issues, including:

- *the nature, gravity and duration of the infringement;*
- *the number of data subjects affected and the level of harm suffered by them;*
- *the intentional or negligent character of the infringement;*

- any action taken by the controller or processor to mitigate the harm;
- any relevant previous infringements by the controller or processor;
- the degree of co-operation with the relevant DPA;
- whether the infringement was self-reported by the controller or processor; and
- any other aggravating or mitigating factors.

By explaining the factors that are relevant to determining the imposition and amount of a fine, the GDPR provides organisations with significantly greater certainty regarding the risk of a fine.

Article 84: Penalties

Penalties and criminal sanctions

For any infringement of EU data protection law that is not subject to administrative fines, Member States may specify additional penalties.

Art.84

Member States set their own rules on penalties applicable to infringements of the GDPR, in particular those infringements that are not subject to administrative fines. Member States may also provide their own rules on criminal sanctions for infringement of the GDPR.

At a practical level, it is likely that there will continue to be some differences between the applications of penalties, due to variations in the national laws of Member States. The possible introduction of criminal sanctions for unlawful processing of personal data presents a significant risk for organisations, depending on how Member States interpret and apply that power.

Chapter 9: Provisions relating to specific data processing

situations

In this Chapter we cover the following Articles:

Article 85: Processing and freedom of expression and information
Article 86: Processing and public access to official documents
Article 87: Processing of the national identification number
Article 88: Processing in the context of employment
Article 89: Safeguards and derogations relating to processing for archiving purposes in the public interest, scientific or historical research purposes or statistical purposes
Article 90: Obligations of secrecy
Article 91: Existing data protection rules of churches and religious associations

Although a key aim of the GDPR is to harmonise data protection law across the EU, there are a number of areas in which the GDPR leaves it to Member States to adopt their own national rules (e.g., because Member States have constitutional rules in these areas, or because these issues fall outside the EU's legislative competence).

Out-of-scope areas of law

The EU does not have the power to legislate on all areas of law. To the extent that EU law does not apply in a particular area, that area is exempt from the provisions of EU data protection law.

Art.2(2)(a)

Any data processing activities that fall outside the scope of EU law are not subject to the GDPR.

Article 85: Processing and freedom of expression and information

Processing of personal data and freedom of expression and information

Member States remain responsible for determining the limits of free expression under their respective national laws. This may mean that data can be processed for the purposes of free expression in some Member States but not others.

Art.17(3), 85

Member states must reconcile the right to protection of personal data under the GDPR with the right to freedom of expression and information, including the processing of personal data for journalistic purposes and the purposes of academic, artistic or literary expression.

Member States remain responsible for determining the balance between the right to privacy and the right to freedom of expression.

Relationship between EU data protection law and freedom of expression

The Directive and the GDPR both leave it to each Member State to determine the right balance in the national context. However, organisations that are involved in the media should carefully consider the fact that the rules in this area will differ from one Member State to the next as each has a differing cultural perspective of the privacy vs. freedom of expression balance.

Article 86: Processing and public access to official documents

Personal data contained in official documents

Member States are responsible for striking a balance between the right to privacy and the need to process personal data where such processing is in the public interest.

Art.86

Personal data contained in official documents may be processed, in order to reconcile public access to official documents with the right to the protection of personal data.

This provision is unlikely to materially affect organisations that do not regularly process personal data contained in official documents.

Article 87: Processing of the national identification number

Processing national ID numbers

Member States are free to set their own rules regarding the processing of national ID numbers.

Art.87

Member States are free to determine the conditions under which national ID numbers may be processed, subject to appropriate safeguards for the rights and freedoms of data subjects pursuant to the GDPR.

The GDPR only adds an obligation to implement appropriate safeguards for the rights and freedoms of data subjects to the existing Directive.

Article 88: Processing in the context of employment

Employment law varies from one Member State to the next, and the rules relating to the EU data protection law and employment law need to be determined at the national level by each Member State.

Processing in the employment context

In most respects, the employment laws of Member States are outside the legislative competence of the EU. Therefore, EU data protection law recognises that each Member State must find its own balance between the right to privacy and the requirements of national employment law.

Art.9(2)(b), 88

Member States may create new laws or conclude collective agreements to ensure the protection of personal data in the context of national employment law. These must include appropriate safeguards. Member States must inform the Commission of any laws adopted in this area.

The GDPR allows for Member States to create laws governing the relationship between the GDPR and national employment law. Organisations however will need to become acquainted with these laws in Member States that apply additional protections to the privacy rights of employees.

Article 89: Safeguards and derogations relating to processing for archiving purposes in the public interest, scientific or historical research purposes or statistical purposes

Processing personal data for scientific, historical or statistical purposes

EU data protection law recognises the fact that there are certain purposes for which personal data may be processed in the public interest, outside of the GDPR's standard requirements.

Art.89(1), (2)

Subject to appropriate safeguards, and provided that there is no risk of breaching the privacy of the data subject, Member States may restrict the data subject's rights to access, rectification, restriction of processing and to object when it comes to the processing of their personal data for scientific, historical or statistical purposes.

Article 90: Obligations of secrecy

Obligations of professional secrecy

Some Member States impose specific obligations of professional secrecy onto organisations in certain sectors (e.g., law firms or banks).

Art.9(2)(i), (3), 14(5)(d), 54(2), 90

Member States may create their own rules in relation to controllers or processors that are subject to obligations of professional secrecy. Member States that adopt such rules must inform the Commission.

In those jurisdictions that have professional secrecy laws, the relationship between those laws and the GDPR like the Directive will be governed by national law.

Article 91: Existing data protection rules of churches and religious associations

Processing personal data in the context of churches and religious establishments

In a number of Member States, membership of a church or other religious establishment can have legal consequences for individuals

Art.91

Where, in a Member State, churches and religious associations or communities impose rules regarding the processing of personal data, such rules may continue to apply, provided that they are brought into line with the provisions of the GDPR. Churches and religious

associations that impose such rules are subject to the oversight of the relevant DPA.

Chapter 10: Delegated Acts and Implementing Acts

In this Chapter we will cover the following Articles:

Article 92: Exercise of the delegation

Delegation of Power

The power to adopt delegated acts is conferred on the Commission subject to the conditions laid down in this Article.

2. The delegation of power referred to in Article 12(8) and Article 43(8) shall be conferred on the Commission for an indeterminate period of time from 24 May 2016.

Article 93: Committee procedure

Assistance of a Committee

The Commission shall be assisted by a committee. That committee shall be a committee within the meaning of Regulation (EU) No 182/2011.

Whereas the Directive is far more verbose and explicit on the makeup of the committee and its role and tasks the GDPR only acknowledges that there shall be a committee but not how it will be composed nor its roles and duties.

Chapter 11: Final provisions

In this Chapter we cover the following Articles:

Article 94: Repeal of Directive 95/46/EC
Article 95: Relationship with Directive 2002/58/EC
Article 96: Relationship with previously concluded Agreements
Article 97: Commission Reports
Article 98: Review of other union legal acts on data protection
Article 99: Entry into force and application

From the GDPR Effective Date 25th May 2018, the GDPR will be the main instrument governing EU data protection law across all Member States.

All types of organisations are affected by the adoption of the GDPR; however, the potential uncertainty regarding the relationship between the GDPR and other laws is likely to be an issue for telecoms providers in particular.

Article 94: Repeal of Directive 95/46/EC

Repeal of the Directive

From the GDPR Effective Date, the Directive will no longer apply in the EU.

Art.94

The GDPR repeals the Directive, with effect from the GDPR Effective Date. From that point on, any references to the Directive will be construed as references to the GDPR, and any references to the WP29 will be construed as references to the EDPB.

The purpose of the GDPR is essentially to replace the Directive. It follows that the Directive must be repealed from the GDPR Effective Date (i.e., 25 May 2018).

Article 95: Relationship with Directive 2002/58/EC

Relationship with the ePrivacy Directive

The ePrivacy Directive provides a specific set of privacy rules to harmonise the processing of personal data by the telecoms sector. Until it is amended, the ePrivacy Directive will co-exist with the GDPR (which applies to all sectors including the telecoms sector).

Art.95

The GDPR does not impose additional obligations on telecoms providers that process personal data under the ePrivacy Directive. However, there remains some uncertainty in the relationship between the ePrivacy Directive and the GDPR, which will require future clarification.

The coexistence of the GDPR alongside the ePrivacy Directive may give rise to uncertainty in the telecoms sector, and requires clarification. The European Commission is currently reviewing the relationship between the GDPR and the ePrivacy Directive and is expected to provide further clarity on this issue.

Article 96: Relationship with previously concluded Agreements

Relationship with existing international agreements

Member states can transfer personal data outside the EU or to an international organisation if there is an international agreement in place that does not prejudice other provisions of EU data protection law and includes an appropriate level of protection for the fundamental rights of the data subject.

Art.48, 96

International agreements involving the transfer of personal data to third countries or international organisations which were concluded by Member States prior to the entry into force of the GDPR, and which are compliant with applicable EU law remain in force until amended, replaced or revoked.

The GDPR does not affect the validity of existing international agreements that have already been concluded by Member States.

Article 97: Commission Reports

Reporting Criteria

By 25 May 2020 and every four years thereafter, the Commission shall submit a report on the evaluation and review of this Regulation to the European Parliament and to the Council. The reports shall be made public.

... the Commission shall examine, in particular, the application and functioning of: (a) Chapter V on the transfer of personal data to third countries or international organisations with particular regard to decisions adopted... (b) Chapter VII on cooperation and consistency.

The GDPR establishes a reporting obligation and an initial timeline and scope for the Commissions reports.

Article 98: Review of other union legal acts on data protection

Review other Union acts relating to the protection of natural persons

The Commission shall, if appropriate, submit legislative proposals with a view to amending other Union legal acts on the protection of personal data, in order to ensure uniform and consistent protection of natural persons with regard to processing. This shall in particular concern the rules relating to the protection of natural persons with regard to processing by Union institutions, bodies, offices and agencies and on the free movement of such data.

Article 99: Entry into force and application

This Regulation will be binding in its entirety and directly applicable in all member states from 26th May 2018

Printed in Great Britain
by Amazon